PASTA

THEO RANDALL

PASTA

EBURY
PRESS

1 3 5 7 9 10 8 6 4 2

Published in 2010 by Ebury Press, an imprint of Ebury Publishing
Ebury Publishing is a division of the Random House Group

Text © Theo Randall 2010
Photography by Vanessa Courtier

Theo Randall has asserted his right to be identified as the author of this Work
in accordance with the Copyright, Designs and Patents Act 1988

The Random House Group Limited Reg. No. 954009

Addresses for companies within the Random House Group can be found at
www.randomhouse.co.uk

A CIP catalogue record for this book is available from the British Library

The Random House Group Limited supports The Forest Stewardship Council (FSC), the leading
international forest certification organisation. All our titles that are printed on Greenpeace approved
FSC certified paper carry the FSC logo. Our paper procurement policy can be found at
www.rbooks.co.uk/environment

Design: Two Associates
Photographer: Vanessa Courtier
Copy editor: Jane Middleton

Printed and bound in China by C&C Offset Printing Co., Ltd

ISBN: 9780091929008

To buy books by your favourite authors and register for offers visit www.rbooks.co.uk

Recipe notes: All recipes serve 4 people as a main course
or 6 people as a starter unless specified otherwise.
When cooking dried pasta, please refer to the cooking time
on the packet (see page 19).

To Natalie,
Max and Lola

CONTENTS

INTRODUCTION

One of the reasons I wanted to write this book was to show how easy it is to make a really good plate of pasta. If you follow the instructions in the recipes and trust your instincts, you will always produce something delicious. Cooking is all about confidence, and the more pasta dishes you prepare the more confident you will become.

Less is definitely more when it comes to cooking pasta. Making sure it is perfectly cooked is more important than how many flavours you have with it. There is nothing better than a simple plate of spaghetti with olive oil, garlic, salt and pepper.

My mother taught me to cook pasta when I was just six years old, and I have adored spaghetti in particular from a very early age. I'll never forget the first time I ate spaghetti alla vongole in Venice. I was only eight but it was a life-changing experience. The combination of the pasta, clams, garlic and parsley was so delicious, and I loved the fact that it was acceptable to use your fingers to take the clams out of their shells. I love cooking pasta for my own children, and on rainy days have been known to set up ravioli-making competitions, which tend to be very messy but great fun. There's a real sense of achievement when you make something to eat from scratch – particularly if you serve it to friends. It also makes for great conversation at dinner.

My first job was for the chef Max Magarian, who owned a French restaurant called Chez Max in Surbiton. He taught me the discipline of preparation and cooking and the importance of simplicity. This was in the middle of the nouvelle cuisine era but Max wasn't having anything to do with it; he believed classic food was the only way. After spending almost four years with Max, I went to work in a little restaurant that had just opened for dinner on the Thames called The River Café, and met two women who went on to change the way we think of Italian food in this country. Working there was an amazing experience, as it had a very different feel from most restaurants in London at the time and also had a great philosophy, not just about food but about life itself.

You can't really understand pasta until you have eaten it in Italy. No matter where you are, the Italians have an understanding of pasta, and it's very rare to be served a bad plateful. I have spent a lot of time in Italy over the years trying great pasta in little trattorias and even some fancy restaurants. I have been so inspired to re-create my experiences there that I buy eggs and flour for the restaurant direct from Italy, just so we can make pasta with the same amazing deep yellow colour that you get in regions such as Piedmont. We aim to reach a comparable level of quality to that in Italy, to the point where we spend eight hours a day making pasta. We always ensure that it is made the day before serving, so it dries out slightly and has the perfect al dente bite.

I'm not alone in my enthusiasm for pasta. It has become a staple food in the UK, and there is a remarkable variety available in the shops. Pasta can be simple or more technical, and it is a great medium for using seasonal ingredients. It can be made by the most experienced cook or by a complete novice. I believe pasta is the first thing that everyone should be taught to cook properly, as once you understand the principles you will enjoy it that much more. The Italians, of course, take pasta very seriously, and quite rightly so. There are different shapes and sauces in every corner of the country, reflecting the region and the produce available. A lot of pasta recipes have peasant origins but in Italy there is no class system where food is concerned – everyone, whether rich or poor, appreciates good pasta.

When you sit down in even the simplest restaurant in Italy, you are always given *antipasti* followed by *primi* and *secondi*. I consider the *primi* course, which consists of pasta or risotto, to be the most important, as it usually gives a good indication of the quality of the restaurant. The portion is always what we would call a starter. This is because, as a rule, pasta shouldn't be served in large quantities. When you eat it, the first mouthful should taste as delicious as the last, but if you have too much on your plate it will congeal as it cools and acquire a slightly unpleasant characteristic. I'm not a fan of main-course pastas but I suspect the reason we eat them in this country is that we don't have a tradition of three courses. Next time you have friends over for dinner, put together some *antipasti* – for example, mozzarella, prosciutto, artichokes, roasted peppers, etc. – then serve a small portion of pasta followed by a simple main course, such as grilled beef or maybe a whole roast fish to share. You will appreciate that you have eaten a very well-balanced meal – vegetables to start, followed by carbohydrate and then protein.

The quantities in this book are for four main-course portions or six starter, or *primi,* portions. I have given smaller quantities for egg pasta than for durum wheat pasta, as dried egg pasta tends to increase more in volume when cooked.

Most of the ingredients in the recipes shouldn't be too difficult to find. If you do have problems tracking down specialist items, try Natoora (www.natoora.co.uk), a supplier I use in the restaurant and at home. They purchase most of their vegetables directly from Italy (including Datterini and Ox Heart tomatoes) and are a good source of cheeses such as burrata, buffalo mozzarella and pecorino.

Finally, the dried pasta I've used in this book is De Cecco and the canned tomatoes Cirio, both of which are available from many major supermarkets and delis and are stocked by Natoora (see above).

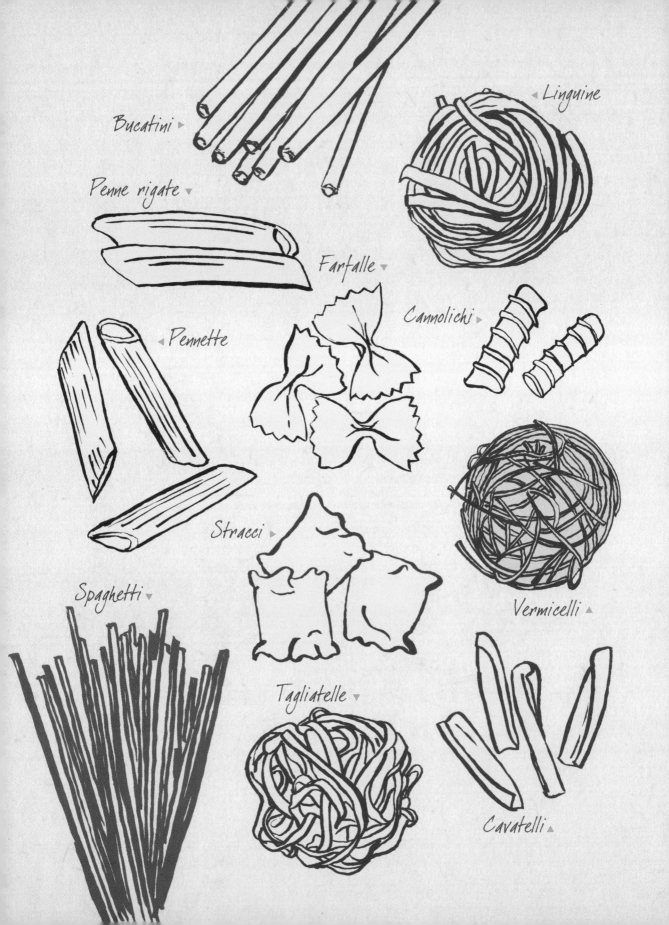

Bucatini ▶

◀ Linguine

Penne rigate ▾

Farfalle ▾

◀ Pennette

Cannolichi ▶

Stracci ▾

Spaghetti ▾

Vermicelli ▶

Tagliatelle ▾

Cavatelli ▶

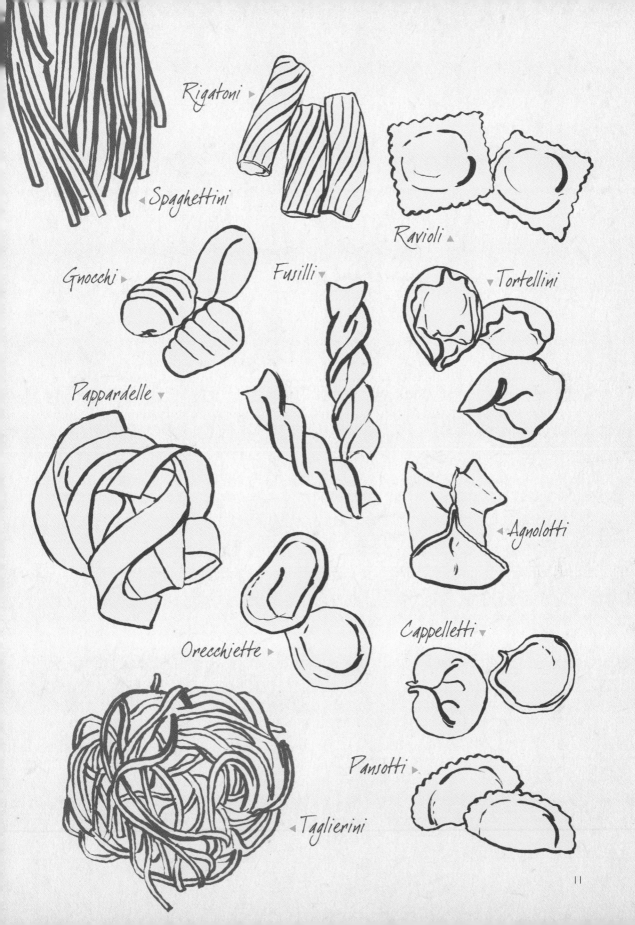

Rigatoni ▶

Spaghettini ◀

Ravioli ▶

Gnocchi ▶

Fusilli ▶

◀ Tortellini

Pappardelle ▼

◀ Agnolotti

Orecchiette ◀

Cappelletti ▼

Pansotti ▼

◀ Taglierini

FRESH PASTA

Fresh pasta is a lot easier to make than most people imagine. The dough doesn't have to be kneaded for ages; you can just whiz the ingredients together in a food processor and it is ready in seconds. Rolling out and cutting the dough is fun and very satisfying to do.

Fresh pasta dough is particularly useful for making stuffed pastas such as ravioli, tortellini and agnolotti. It is very pliable, so you can use it for all manner of shapes and sizes. Stuffed pastas tend to be served on the day on which they are made (though you can store them in the fridge for a couple of days if necessary), but ribbon pastas such as taglierini, tagliatelle and pappardelle are best made a day in advance so they dry out slightly. This results in a much firmer texture when cooked, which enables them to absorb the sauce better. If you cook them straight away, they can be quite slimy.

The key to success when making pasta dough is to use good-quality eggs and the correct proportion of egg to flour. I find the best eggs are Italian ones. They have much richer yolks than most of the eggs you can buy in the UK, since the chickens are fed a diet of corn and carrots, which enhances the colour and texture of the yolk. However, any good organic eggs would be fine. If you keep your own hens, try hanging up a bunch of carrots for them to peck.

The flour should be Italian tipo 00 flour – a very fine flour that is now available in many large supermarkets. Apart from this, all you need is a little fine semolina flour and your eggs. Don't add salt or olive oil to the dough; they will do nothing except discolour it.

You will need to invest in a pasta machine for rolling out the dough. They can be bought in any good kitchen shop. The best ones, of course, are Italian, and my favourite brand is Imperia. The small ones are ideal for home cooks. If you are a bit more ambitious, Imperia also makes a restaurant machine, which is probably the best pasta machine you can buy. The manual machines (as opposed to the electric ones) tend to be the safest and the nicest to use, because you can work at your own pace rather than the speed of the rollers.

A pasta machine not only rolls out the pasta dough and cuts it if necessary, it also 'proves' the dough, which is vital to ensure a good texture. It's a simple process of feeding the dough through the rollers at their widest setting at least five times, folding it in three between each rolling. This works the gluten in the flour and gives the dough elasticity, enabling you to roll it out quite finely.

Finally, don't feel you have to make your own pasta in order to cook the recipes in this book. There are some good brands of dried egg pasta available, including Pasta del Aldo and Cipriani.

Pasta Dough

300g tipo 00 flour
100g fine semolina, plus extra for dusting
2 large organic eggs
6 large organic egg yolks

Place all the ingredients in a food processor and pulse until they form a yellow ball of dough. At this point, the dough should have a smooth, firm but slightly sticky texture, almost like plasticine. If it seems wet, add an extra teaspoon or two of flour. Divide the dough into 2 equal balls and immediately wrap them in cling film to prevent them drying out. The dough will keep in the fridge for up to 10 days. You can freeze it but I wouldn't recommend it, since it can discolour and lose a lot of moisture on thawing.

Proving and rolling out the dough

With the rollers of your pasta machine on their widest setting, pass a piece of dough through, then fold it into 3. Give it a quarter turn and pass it through the machine again. Repeat this 5 or 6 times so the gluten in the pasta is thoroughly worked, then pass it through the machine to roll it out, progressively narrowing the rollers by one notch each time. Make it as thin as you feel comfortable with. The more the pasta has been worked initially, the thinner you will be able to roll it. Make sure the pasta sheet is no more than 60cm long, otherwise it will be difficult to handle and may break.

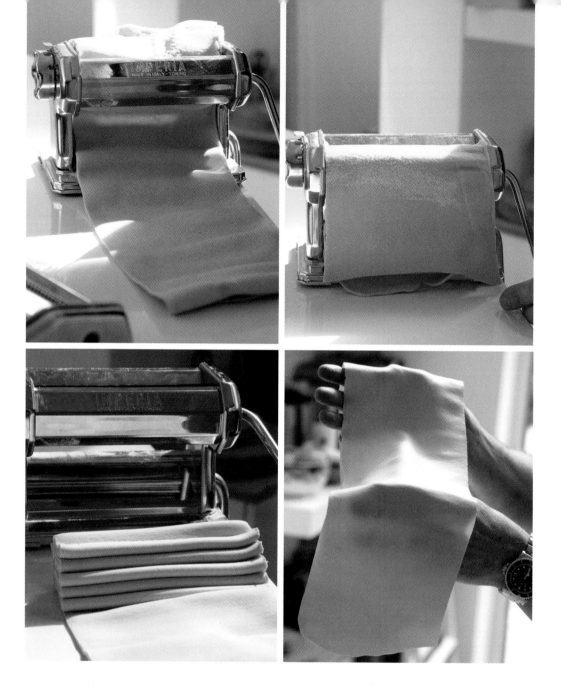

Cutting the dough

Once you have a long piece of very thin pasta, use the cutters on your machine to cut it into taglierini, tagliatelle or pappardelle. Place the cut pasta on a long tray in a single layer, sprinkling it lightly with semolina flour so it doesn't stick. Cover with greaseproof paper and leave in the fridge overnight. This will help dry out the pasta and give a better texture once it is cooked. Alternatively you could put it on a wire rack and leave to dry at room temperature for 12 hours. The pasta should be firm but not too brittle; if it's brittle it will break when you pick it up, and that's the last thing you want.

STUFFED PASTA

Making ravioli

Roll out the pasta dough as thinly as possible, in a sheet about 12cm wide and 60cm long.

Place heaped teaspoonfuls of the filling along the length of the pasta, leaving a 3cm gap between each one and making sure there is enough pasta free to fold over the filling.

Brush a little water between each pile of filling, then fold the pasta over and, using your 2 little fingers, push down round each ravioli to seal. Try to ensure that there is no trapped air inside.

With a ridged ravioli cutter or a sharp knife, cut between each ravioli and trim off any overlapping pasta. The ravioli can be cooked straight away or kept in the fridge on a floured tray for up to 2 days

Making agnolotti

Roll out the pasta dough as thinly as possible, in a sheet 60cm long and 12cm wide.

Cut it lengthwise in half, then cut it across at 6cm intervals so you end up with 6cm squares of pasta.

Put a heaped teaspoon of filling in the middle of each square, then brush the edges with a little water.

Bring 2 opposite corners up to meet in the middle, then bring up the remaining 2 corners, forming a diamond shape. Make sure all the sides are sealed and there is no excess air inside. The agnolotti should look a bit like Chinese paper lanterns.

Put the agnolotti in the fridge on a floured tray until you are ready to cook them. You can prepare them up to 2 days in advance, as long as the filling is not too wet.

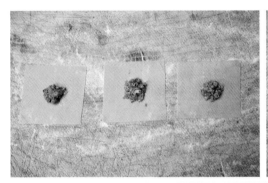

Potato Gnocchi

Gnocchi follows the same principle as pasta except it includes potato, which makes it much lighter. The fresher it is, the better it tastes. There are some good bought varieties available but when you have a bit of time, try making your own. The flavour of home-made gnocchi is unique, and generally a lot lighter in texture than the manufactured variety. It is real comfort food and goes well with virtually any kind of sauce.

1kg floury potatoes, peeled and cut in half
200g tipo 00 flour
2 large organic egg yolks

Cook the potatoes in boiling salted water until really tender. Drain through a colander and leave for a few minutes so the excess moisture steams off. Mash through a mouli-légumes, or use a potato ricer or masher, making sure there are no lumps. Place in a bowl and leave to cool.

Mix the flour into the cold mash, then add the egg yolks and beat together, forming a soft dough.

Divide into 6 pieces and, using the palms of your hands and your fingertips, roll each one into a long sausage about 2cm in diameter. Cut into 2cm lengths, then push each one gently over the back of a fork on to a floured board. This gives the gnocchi a few ridges and a crevice, which will help to hold the sauce, making them really tasty.

Carefully place the gnocchi in a large pan of well-salted boiling water and cook until they rise to the top. This shouldn't take more than about 2 minutes. Remove with a slotted spoon and serve straight away. For a real treat, toss them with butter and grated Parmesan and grate over a truffle, if possible a white one.

DRIED PASTA

Dried pasta has a very different texture and flavour from fresh pasta. It is neither better nor worse, but simply has a different usage – clams cooked with white wine, garlic and parsley, for example, work much better with spaghetti than with fresh pasta; on the other hand, fresh pasta, particularly tagliatelle, tastes really delicious with just butter and Parmesan.

The best dried pastas are pushed through bronze dyes during production to give a rougher texture, enabling them to absorb the sauce when cooked. These pastas are labelled artisan and often come in paper packages with an elaborate design. Some of them can be very overpriced. I find the most reliable, and most forgiving, is De Cecco, which is available practically everywhere. De Cecco also produces one of the largest ranges of shapes and sizes, with a pasta for every sauce. Avoid quick-cook pasta, as it is made with inferior-quality flour, which does not produce the correct *al dente* texture.

Cooking and serving pasta

It's a good idea to measure out your pasta before cooking; if you cook more than you need, it alters the ratio of pasta to sauce, effectively diluting the sauce. Pasta should be cooked in plenty of water so it can move around freely and doesn't clump together – 400g dried pasta, or 250g fresh, needs at least 4 litres of water and a teaspoon of good-quality sea salt. Bring the salted water to a rolling boil, then sprinkle in the pasta so it won't stick together in a lump. Stir after a couple of minutes to prevent sticking.

When the pasta is slightly undercooked – say, 2 minutes away from the recommended cooking time on the pack for dried pasta – drain it, holding back a little of the cooking water, and add it to the sauce (if the pan in which you made the sauce is too small to hold the pasta, transfer the sauce to a large warmed frying pan while the pasta is cooking). Heat gently for a couple of minutes, so the pasta carries on cooking and also absorbs all the flavours of the sauce. At this point the pasta and sauce should be tossed together vigorously. This will give you well-lubricated pasta that doesn't stick together. If the sauce seems a little thick, use some of the reserved cooking water to adjust the consistency; this will make the pasta easier to toss.

Always serve pasta straight away, piping hot, in warmed plates or bowls. I prefer to use bowls because they keep it hot and also if you have a little extra sauce or juice it sits nicely in the bowl.

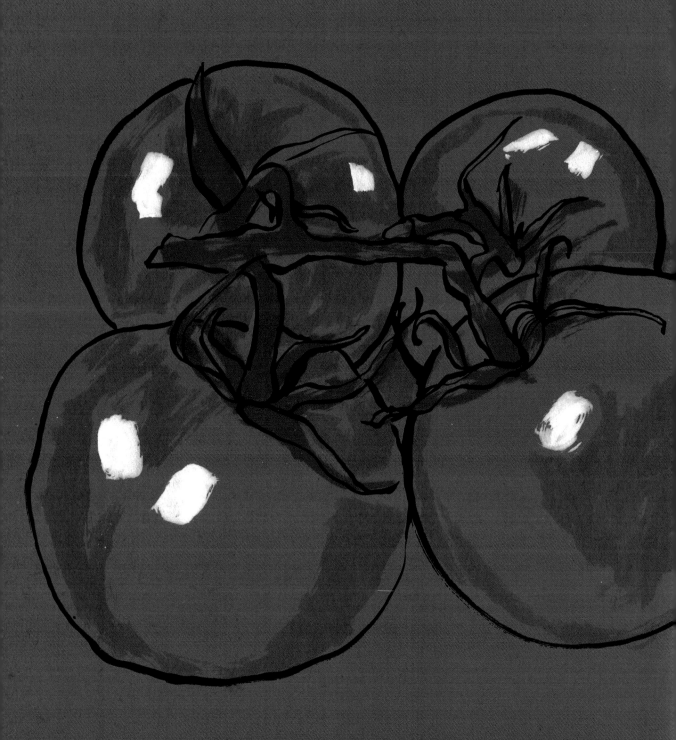

Tomatoes

Tomatoes

In summer, there is nothing better than ripe plum tomatoes for making a really delicious fresh tomato sauce. But, as with lots of Italian food, when ingredients are at their best they tend to be preserved, so good-quality canned tomatoes can work equally well. The best tomatoes I've come across for cooking are San Marzano. They have few seeds, which means they are low in acidity and very fleshy. It's always worth spending money on decent tomatoes, whether fresh or canned, because they often form the main part of the pasta sauce.

The most important thing about a fresh tomato is its ripeness. A ripe tomato should be like a peach; if you squeeze it, it should give a little, and when you cut it open it should smell almost sweet. In pasta sauces, fresh tomatoes are useful not only as a sauce in themselves but in smaller quantities to highlight the main ingredient.

There are so many varieties of tomato, from the widely available plum and cherry tomatoes to lesser known ones such as the delicious Datterini and Ox Heart – two of my favourites for pasta sauces (if you can't find them in supermarkets, you can buy Datterini tomatoes online from www.natoora.co.uk). Supermarkets stock many different kinds, but beware: some of them can be unripe and pretty tasteless. Try to buy tomatoes that have been produced in Italy, Spain or France, as these are most likely to have been grown in a natural environment, which will enhance their flavour.

The best tomatoes of all are probably the ones you grow yourself. Failing that, try farmers' markets and street markets. Always ask the trader if you can have the ripest tomatoes – even overripe, squashy tomatoes make great sauce. If you have too many, make a large batch of tomato sauce (see page 27) and store it in the fridge for up to a week or in the freezer.

Tomatoes are very much a seasonal ingredient, but we long for them all year round. So when it's cold and dark, substitute good-quality canned – or, better still, bottled – tomatoes for fresh ones. Tomatoes preserved in jars tend to have been picked ripe, then blanched and bottled on the farm, in their natural juice with no additives (if you do buy a big box of tomatoes in a market, you can preserve them this way yourself at home). The problem with most canned tomatoes is that they have often been picked unripe and are kept in tomato purée, so when cooking them you get the flavour of the purée rather than the tomato. The seeds tend to be green and very acidic, giving a rather unpleasant sauce. The best way to avoid this is to buy chopped Italian tomatoes in cans. These are usually picked ripe as it makes them easier to chop.

Pappardelle with Roasted Datterini Tomatoes, Taggiasche Olives and Basil

Like cherry tomatoes, Datterini have a high acidity, which turns to sweetness when ripe. If you remove the seeds, the tomatoes will be even sweeter, as it is the seeds that contain the bitter tannins. This dish combines the saltiness of olives and the sweetness of tomatoes with garlic, basil and olive oil. It's very important to add the cooked pasta to the roasting dish, so you can get every last trace of juice from it.

If you can't find Datterini tomatoes, use good cherry tomatoes instead.

500g Datterini tomatoes
2 garlic cloves, finely sliced
75g Taggiasche olives, stoned
a small bunch of basil
3 tablespoons olive oil
250g fresh pappardelle (or dried egg pappardelle)
75g young pecorino cheese, grated
sea salt and freshly ground black pepper

Cut the tomatoes in half widthways and squeeze out the seeds. Put the tomatoes in a bowl and toss with the garlic, olives, half the basil, torn into small pieces, 2 tablespoons of the olive oil and some salt and pepper. Transfer to a roasting tin or an ovenproof dish and place in an oven preheated to 190°C/Gas Mark 5. Roast for 20 minutes; the tomatoes will break up slightly but this is a good thing. Most importantly, their flavour will be concentrated. Remove from the oven and leave to stand for a few minutes.

Cook the pappardelle in a large pan of boiling salted water for 3–4 minutes, until *al dente* (or cook according to the packet instructions for dried pappardelle). Drain and add to the tomato mixture. Add the remaining tablespoon of olive oil, then rip up the remaining basil and add that too. Toss together until the pasta is coated in the tomato juices. Serve immediately, with the grated pecorino and some black pepper.

Spaghetti with Fresh Tomato Sauce

This is a basic sauce to which you can add other ingredients, such as shellfish. On its own, it is one of the all-time greats.

A fresh tomato sauce should be made very quickly – the longer you cook a tomato, the more flavour it will lose. Always use ripe plum tomatoes, which are very fleshy and not too acidic.

250g ripe plum tomatoes
1 tablespoon olive oil
1 garlic clove, finely sliced
1 teaspoon chopped basil
400g spaghetti
sea salt and freshly ground black pepper

Put the tomatoes in a bowl of boiling water for 1 minute, then transfer to a bowl of cold water. Peel off the skins, cut the tomatoes in half and remove the seeds, then chop the flesh. Place in a colander, sprinkle with sea salt and leave for 10 minutes. This will remove excess water.

Heat the olive oil in a large shallow pan, add the garlic and sweat until soft. Throw in the tomatoes and cook quickly over a fairly high heat to retain their natural flavour – about 5 minutes should do it. The sauce should be quite loose but not watery. Stir in the basil and adjust the seasoning.

Cook the pasta in a large pan of boiling salted water until *al dente*, then drain. Add to the sauce, toss together gently for a couple of minutes over a low heat, then serve.

Spaghettini with Tomato and Anchovy Sauce

This is the pasta to cook on the first day of your holiday in Italy, when you've just arrived and the only shop open is a tiny grocer's. They will always have anchovies in jars, canned tomatoes and, of course, a huge selection of spaghetti. If you're lucky, they might even have some good-quality pine nuts.

1 tablespoon olive oil
1 garlic clove, finely sliced
8 salted anchovy fillets in olive oil
a pinch of dried chilli flakes
400g can of chopped tomatoes
400g spaghettini
2 tablespoons pine nuts (preferably European ones), toasted
1 tablespoon chopped flat-leaf parsley
sea salt and freshly ground black pepper

Heat the olive oil in a large, heavy-based saucepan and add the garlic and anchovy fillets. Cook gently for 2 minutes, stirring, until the anchovy fillets have dissolved into the oil. Add the dried chilli and then the tomatoes. Bring to a simmer and cook over a low heat for 20–25 minutes, until the sauce is thick and concentrated. Season to taste.

Cook the spaghettini in a large pan of boiling salted water until *al dente*, then drain and add to the sauce. Toss well and cook over a low heat for a couple of minutes. Add the toasted pine nuts and chopped parsley and toss again. Serve with black pepper and maybe a little drizzle of really good olive oil.

Penne with Fresh Plum Tomatoes, Borlotti Beans and Basil

It's important to buy good-quality borlotti beans for this dish. The ones in jars are superior to canned beans and aren't that much more expensive. They are available from most good delis and even some supermarkets.

200g fresh plum tomatoes
2 tablespoons olive oil, plus extra to serve
1 garlic clove, finely sliced
a pinch of dried chilli flakes
1 jar of borlotti beans, drained
2 tablespoons chopped basil
400g penne rigate
sea salt and freshly ground black pepper

Put the tomatoes in a bowl of boiling water for 1 minute, then transfer to a bowl of cold water. Peel off the skins, cut the tomatoes in half and remove the seeds, then finely chop the flesh.

Heat the olive oil in a large frying pan, add the garlic and cook until softened. Add the dried chilli and chopped tomatoes and cook for about 10 minutes, until the tomatoes have reduced in volume by half. Add the drained borlotti beans and cook for a further 5 minutes. Stir in the chopped basil and season to taste.

Cook the penne in a large pan of boiling salted water until *al dente*, then drain and add to the sauce. Toss well together and cook gently for 2 minutes, then serve with a good drizzle of olive oil and some black pepper.

Bucatini with Tomato and Pancetta Sauce

You will find this classic dish in virtually every restaurant in Rome. Its simplicity is what makes it so special. It's one of those really warm, filling pasta dishes that you crave on cold winter days.

3 tablespoons olive oil
100g pancetta, cut into fine matchsticks
1 small red onion, chopped
1 dried red chilli, deseeded
400g can of chopped tomatoes
400g bucatini
sea salt and freshly ground black pepper
grated pecorino romano cheese, to serve

Heat the oil in a heavy-based saucepan, add the pancetta and red onion and cook slowly for 10 minutes or until the pancetta has turned a light golden brown and the onion is soft. Add the red chilli and chopped tomatoes, then simmer for 30 minutes, until the sauce is reduced and thick. Season to taste.

Cook the bucatini in a large pan of boiling salted water until *al dente* and then drain. Add to the sauce, toss well and cook over a low heat for 2 minutes. Serve with black pepper and grated pecorino.

Penne all'Arrabbiata

Arrabbiata means angry, but a good arrabbiata shouldn't be angry – it should be spicy and sweet at the same time. Always try to use small, fresh chillies. They will give a much sweeter-tasting heat than the dried variety, which can be super-hot and have a slight astringency.

4 tablespoons olive oil
3 garlic cloves, cut in half
2 red chillies
2 x 400g cans of chopped tomatoes
8 basil leaves, torn
400g penne rigate
sea salt and freshly ground black pepper

Heat the olive oil in a large, heavy-based frying pan, add the garlic and the whole chillies and cook until the garlic is golden brown and the chillies have changed colour. Take out the garlic and chillies and keep to one side. Add the tomatoes to the pan, bring to a simmer and cook over a medium heat for about 20 minutes, until reduced and thickened. Return the chillies and garlic to the pan, season to taste and add the torn basil.

Cook the penne in a large pan of boiling salted water until *al dente*, then drain. Add to the sauce, toss well and cook gently for a couple of minutes. Serve with black pepper and maybe a dash of good, fruity olive oil.

Spaghetti with Ox Heart Tomatoes, Capers, Rocket and Balsamic Vinegar

Ox Heart tomatoes have virtually no seeds, so are very low in acidity. When chopped and salted, they release all their water. They work perfectly in this dish, and are also excellent simply tossed with spaghetti and fresh oregano to make the most delicious summer pasta. If you can't get Ox Heart tomatoes, use ripe beef tomatoes instead.

2 large, ripe Ox Heart tomatoes
2 tablespoons good olive oil
1 teaspoon aged balsamic vinegar
1 tablespoon capers in vinegar, drained
100g wild rocket, roughly chopped
400g spaghetti
75g ricotta salata, grated
sea salt and freshly ground black pepper

Put the tomatoes in a pan of boiling water for 1 minute, then transfer to a bowl of cold water. Peel off the skins, cut the tomatoes in half and remove the seeds. Finely chop the flesh into a pulp and put it into a large bowl. Add the olive oil, balsamic vinegar, capers and chopped rocket, then season well with sea salt and black pepper.

Cook the spaghetti in a large pan of boiling, salted water until *al dente*. Drain and add to the bowl with the marinated tomatoes. Toss well and serve with a good grating of ricotta salata.

Tagliatelle with Slow-cooked Tomato and Basil Sauce

This has got to be the ultimate in pasta sauces. It's just what I want after a busy day in the restaurant. You don't need Parmesan here – just good olive oil and black pepper.

3 tablespoons olive oil
2 garlic cloves, finely sliced
2 x 400g cans of chopped tomatoes
10 basil leaves
250g fresh tagliatelle (or dried egg tagliatelle)
sea salt and freshly ground black pepper
some very good, spicy olive oil, to serve

Heat the olive oil in a large frying pan, add the garlic and cook very gently until translucent. Stir in the chopped tomatoes and cook slowly for 30–40 minutes. When the sauce has become very thick, rip the basil leaves and stir them in. Season to taste.

Cook the tagliatelle in a large pan of boiling salted water for about 3 minutes, until *al dente* (or cook according to the packet instructions for dried tagliatelle). Drain and add to the sauce, then toss well and cook gently for 2 minutes. Finish with a drizzle of spicy olive oil and some black pepper.

Spaghetti with Canned Tomato Sauce

It doesn't matter where you are, every corner shop will have a can of tomatoes and a pack of spaghetti. They're far better for you than a takeaway, and taste much better too.

If you are using whole canned tomatoes, it's worth cutting them in half and removing the seeds. The seeds contain tannins that are released when cooked, making the sauce acidic.

2 tablespoons olive oil
1 garlic clove, finely sliced
400g can of chopped tomatoes
400g spaghetti
sea salt and freshly ground black pepper

Heat the olive oil in a saucepan, add the garlic and sweat until softened. Add the tomatoes and cook slowly for 25 minutes, until thick and creamy. This should give the sauce a sweet taste, as cooking canned tomatoes quickly tends to make them taste acidic.

Cook the pasta in a large pan of boiling salted water until *al dente*, then drain. Add to the sauce, toss together gently for a couple of minutes over a low heat, then serve.

Rigatoni with Tomatoes, Ricotta Salata and Basil

The quantity of tomatoes is quite considerable here, but when cooked slowly they reduce to give a rich, intense flavour that is perfect with the salty ricotta salata cheese.

3 tablespoons olive oil
1 garlic clove, finely sliced
2 x 400g cans of chopped tomatoes
8 basil leaves
400g rigatoni
100g ricotta salata cheese
sea salt and freshly ground black pepper
good olive oil, to serve

Heat the olive oil in a large frying pan, add the garlic and cook gently for 2 minutes, until softened. Add the tomatoes and cook over a medium heat for 30 minutes, until reduced and thickened. Rip up the basil and stir it in. Season with salt and pepper.

Cook the rigatoni in a large pan of boiling salted water until *al dente*, then drain. Add to the tomato sauce, toss well and cook over a low heat for 2 minutes. Finish with some good olive oil and generous gratings of ricotta salata.

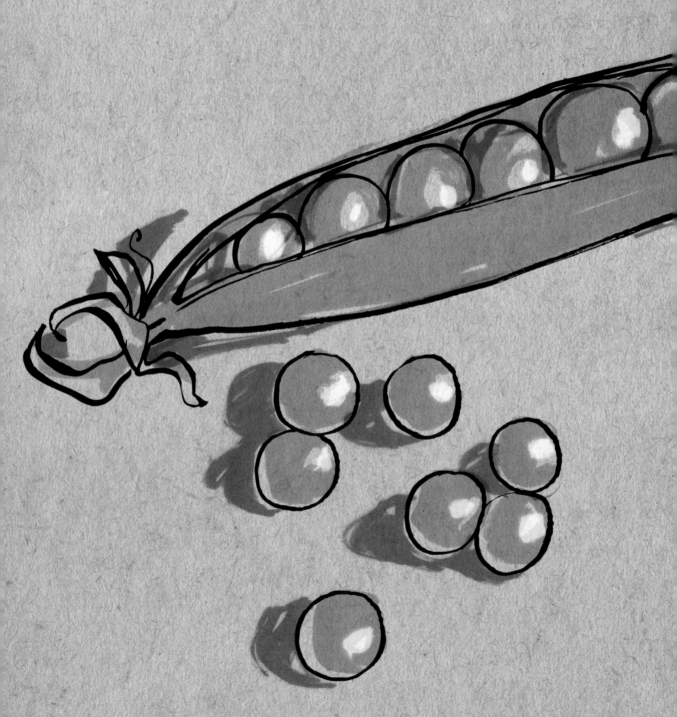

Vegetables

Vegetables

It's hard to imagine pasta dishes without vegetables. In Italy, both pasta and vegetables are very regional, and this creates an enormous variety of dishes. One of my favourite vegetables is the artichoke. There are many different kinds, each of which is served with pasta in a particular style – for example, the large, dense Roman artichokes are very good for slow cooking, particularly as the stem is just as prized as the heart. The first of the season's violet artichokes, which have no choke because they are so young, are wonderful served with a delicate pasta such as taglierini.

Vegetables can give a very seasonal feel to pasta dishes. In springtime, for instance, I like to use young peas and broad beans to make fresh, sweet-tasting sauces. In winter, something as robust and fresh as cavolo nero, combined with new season's olive oil, makes a delightful sauce. In summer, the sunshine brings fabulous treats such as red and yellow peppers – not the smooth, even-shaped peppers you find in supermarkets all year round but knobbly, shiny, brightly coloured peppers that have actually been grown in the sun – or the large, round, purple aubergines that come from southern Italy and have no seeds, making them very dense and sweet.

Probably one of the best vegetables we grow in the UK is asparagus, which is in season in April and May and, when cooked very fresh, has a brilliant colour, texture and flavour. Try it with spaghetti, anchovies, basil and pangrattato (see page 46). The combination of anchovy and crisp breadcrumbs brings out the true texture of the asparagus and highlights its flavour.

Fresh spinach is available all year round. It is very easy to cook and, as most spinach these days is packaged and ready to use, it is ideal for a quick dinner. If you can buy loose spinach, however, it has a lot more flavour and is well worth the extra time spent preparing it.

In the autumn, look out for fantastic squashes – crown prince, onion squash and the butternut squash, which is available all year round, though not from this country. When peeled and roasted, these orange-fleshed vegetables have a remarkable sweetness. Mix them with something as simple as mascarpone or ricotta cheese and you have a delicious filling for any pasta. Also at this time of year, you can find various types of radicchio. A lot of people find them hard to understand, because they can be very bitter. Cooked in the correct way, however, with the addition of something like pancetta, cream and a squeeze of lemon, this bitter vegetable is transformed into a luxurious, bitter-sweet, bright-red sauce that is perfect with fresh or dried pasta.

Spaghetti with Zucchini, Tomatoes, Mozzarella and Sage

Sage is probably the odd ingredient in this recipe. It has an almost medicinal quality when cooked, which adds a huge depth of flavour to the zucchini and tomato without overpowering them.

3 tablespoons olive oil
1 onion, finely sliced
1 garlic clove, finely sliced
4 sage leaves, finely chopped
a pinch of dried chilli flakes
2 medium-sized zucchini, finely sliced
200g plum tomatoes, skinned, deseeded and diced
400g spaghetti
150g buffalo mozzarella, cut into 1cm cubes
sea salt and freshly ground black pepper
good olive oil, to serve
grated Parmesan or, better still, pecorino cheese, to serve (optional)

Heat the olive oil in a frying pan, add the onion and garlic and cook gently for 10 minutes or until really soft. Add the sage, dried chilli and zucchini and cook for 2–3 minutes longer. Add the tomatoes, turn up the heat and cook rapidly for 5–7 minutes, until they have reduced to a thickish consistency. Season to taste.

Cook the spaghetti in a large pan of boiling salted water until *al dente*, then drain. Add to the zucchini mixture, toss well together, then add the mozzarella bit by bit, tossing the pasta as you do so. Check the seasoning and serve with a dash of good olive oil and, if you wish, some grated Parmesan or pecorino.

Rigatoni with Peas, Artichokes, Broad Beans and Prosciutto

The word *primavera* comes to mind with this dish. It's a celebration of spring, as all the ingredients are at their best at this time of year.

2 artichokes
juice of 1 lemon
2 tablespoons olive oil
1 spring onion, finely chopped
1 garlic clove, finely sliced
150g podded peas
150g podded broad beans
100ml water
4 slices of Parma ham, cut into strips
1 tablespoon chopped flat-leaf parsley
75g unsalted butter
400g rigatoni
75g Parmesan cheese, freshly grated
sea salt and freshly ground black pepper

Using a small, sharp knife, trim off the tough outer leaves of the artichokes, exposing the tender, yellowy leaves underneath. Slice off the top 2cm of each artichoke. Peel the stalk with a potato peeler, removing all the green, bitter parts. Take a teaspoon or soupspoon, depending on size, and scoop out the choke. If the artichokes are young, the chokes will be very small; if old, they will be large and quite furry. Place the artichokes in a bowl of water acidulated with the lemon juice to prevent discoloration. Leave for a few minutes, then cut each artichoke lengthwise in half and each half lengthwise into eighths.

Heat the olive oil in a saucepan, add the spring onion and garlic and cook gently until soft. Add the artichokes, peas, broad beans and water, cover with a tight-fitting lid and cook on a medium heat for 15 minutes or until the vegetables are very tender. Stir in the Parma ham, chopped parsley and the butter and season with salt and pepper.

Cook the rigatoni in a large pan of boiling salted water until *al dente*, then drain, reserving a few spoonfuls of the cooking water. Add the pasta to the vegetables, toss together and cook over a low heat for a couple of minutes, adding a tablespoon or so of the reserved pasta water to loosen the sauce. Finish with the grated Parmesan. Toss well and serve with black pepper.

Spaghetti with Asparagus, Anchovies, Basil and Pangrattato

Pangrattato is used in some parts of Italy as an alternative to Parmesan, even though it is not a cheese but deep-fried breadcrumbs. It can be served with most dry or non-tomato sauces but I find that its lovely texture works particularly well with anchovies.

250g asparagus, ends trimmed
130ml olive oil
1 teacup of fresh breadcrumbs
1 garlic clove, finely sliced
5 salted anchovy fillets in olive oil
8 basil leaves, torn
100ml double cream
400g spaghetti
sea salt and freshly ground black pepper

Cook the asparagus in a large pan of boiling salted water until tender, then drain and leave to cool. Cut into slices 1cm thick, at a slight angle. Keep to one side.

Heat 100ml of the olive oil to about 170°C in a small saucepan. Add the breadcrumbs and fry until golden brown. Remove with a slotted spoon, drain on kitchen paper and season with salt and pepper.

Heat the remaining olive oil in a large frying pan, add the garlic and cook gently until softened. Add the anchovy fillets and cook, stirring, until they have dissolved into the oil. Add the asparagus, basil and double cream, cook gently for 3–4 minutes, then season to taste.

Cook the spaghetti in a large pan of boiling salted water until *al dente,* then drain, reserving a few spoonfuls of the cooking water. Add the pasta to the asparagus sauce and toss well, adding a little of the reserved cooking water if necessary to loosen the sauce. Cook gently for a couple of minutes, then serve with the fried breadcrumbs on top.

Farfalle with Broccoli, Anchovies, Chilli, Cream and Parmesan

Broccoli, anchovy and chilli are a classic combination, and adding a little cream ensures that the sauce coats the farfalle nicely. Be sure to use the whole head of broccoli. People often throw the stem away but, when peeled, it can be very tender and sweet.

You could substitute 100g pancetta for the anchovies, if you prefer.

300g broccoli
1 tablespoon olive oil
1 garlic clove, finely sliced
6 salted anchovy fillets in olive oil
1 red chilli, deseeded and finely chopped
100ml double cream
400g farfalle
100g Parmesan cheese, freshly grated
sea salt and freshly ground black pepper

Separate the broccoli florets, then peel the stem and slice it thinly. Cook in a pan of boiling salted water until a knife slips through the broccoli easily. Drain, reserving some of the cooking water.

Heat the olive oil in a frying pan, add the garlic and cook gently until softened. Add the anchovies and chilli and cook, stirring, for a minute or so until the anchovies dissolve into the oil. Stir in the cooked broccoli, then add the cream and 3 tablespoons of the broccoli cooking water. Simmer over a low heat for 10 minutes, then season to taste. Add a little more water if the sauce looks too dry.

Cook the farfalle in a large pan of boiling salted water until *al dente*, then drain, reserving a few spoonfuls of the cooking water. Add to the sauce and toss well, adding a little of the reserved cooking water to loosen the sauce if necessary. Cook gently for a minute or two, then add half the grated Parmesan and toss again. Serve with the remaining Parmesan and some black pepper.

Ravioli with Butternut Squash, Marjoram and Sage

This is the first pasta of autumn. The flavour of the squash combined with the garlic, marjoram and mascarpone makes a sweet yet savoury dish, while the sage butter gives it an extra edge. You could substitute other squashes, such as onion squash or crown prince.

It's very important to serve this with black pepper and Parmesan.

1 small butternut squash, peeled, deseeded and cut into small dice
125g unsalted butter
1 garlic clove, sliced
1 tablespoon chopped marjoram
100g mascarpone cheese
¼ nutmeg, grated
½ quantity of Pasta Dough (see page 13)
a bunch of sage, roughly chopped
sea salt and freshly ground black pepper
freshly grated Parmesan cheese, to serve

Cook the diced butternut squash in boiling salted water until tender, then drain through a colander and leave to cool. The steam from the squash should remove any excess water.

Heat half the butter in a pan, add the garlic and cook gently until softened. Add the marjoram and butternut squash, mash the squash with a wooden spoon and cook for about 10 minutes or until the mixture appears quite dry. Add the mascarpone, grated nutmeg and some seasoning, then leave to cool.

Roll out the pasta dough and make the ravioli as described on page 16. Add the ravioli to a large pan of boiling salted water and simmer for 3–5 minutes, until *al dente*. Meanwhile, soften the remaining butter in a large frying pan, but don't let it melt completely. Add the sage. Drain the ravioli and toss with the butter and sage. Serve in bowls, with black pepper and grated Parmesan.

Linguine with Pesto, Potatoes and Green Beans

Serving pesto with potatoes and green beans is traditional around Genoa. The combination of potato and pasta may seem a bit odd but mixing two carbohydrates, particularly waxy potatoes, works very well with a herby sauce such as pesto.

400g linguine
4 small, waxy potatoes, peeled and sliced about 1mm thick
150g fine green beans, trimmed
1 quantity of Pesto (see page 207)
sea salt and freshly ground black pepper
freshly grated Parmesan cheese, to serve

Add the linguine to a large pan of boiling salted water and cook until *al dente*, adding the potatoes and beans after 4 minutes. If you like your green beans crunchy, put them in a bit later but always add the potatoes after 4 minutes – there is nothing worse than undercooked potato.

Place a large frying pan over the heat so that it is warm – not too hot. Drain the pasta and vegetables, reserving a little of the cooking water, and add them to the frying pan with the pesto. Toss well so the pesto coats the pasta, beans and potatoes, adding a little of the pasta cooking water if necessary to loosen the sauce. Adjust the seasoning, then serve with grated Parmesan, plus a little extra pesto on top if there is any left.

Pappardelle with Cavolo Nero and New Season's Olive Oil

This is a very simple sauce, using dark green cavolo nero, or black cabbage, and spicy, new-season olive oil, which is available after the first pressing in November. In the UK, with a little bit of research, you can now find new season's olive oil fairly easily. Tuscan oils, which would traditionally be used in this recipe, tend to be the spiciest and greenest of all, while the southern Italian oils are softer and grassier.

3 bunches of cavolo nero (about 600g), stems discarded
3 garlic cloves, peeled
100ml new season's olive oil
250g fresh pappardelle (or dried egg pappardelle)
sea salt and freshly ground black pepper
freshly grated Parmesan, to serve (optional)

Blanch the cavolo nero and garlic cloves in plenty of boiling salted water for about 5 minutes, until the garlic is tender. Remove the cavolo nero and garlic from the pan with a slotted spoon but keep the water. Put the cabbage and garlic in a blender or food processor and blitz with enough of the cooking water to give a thick, smooth purée (be careful not to add too much water). Season with salt and pepper and then mix in the olive oil. Transfer to a saucepan and heat gently.

Cook the pappardelle in a large pan of boiling salted water for 3–4 minutes, until *al dente* (or cook according to the packet instructions for dried pappardelle). Drain, reserving a few spoonfuls of the cooking water, and add to the warm cavolo nero sauce. Toss well, adding a little of the reserved cooking water if necessary to loosen the sauce. Heat gently for 2 minutes before serving. It's good without the Parmesan, but it's also good with it!

Tagliatelle with Aubergines, Tomato and Basil

This kind of sauce is normally associated with dried pasta. It works really well with tagliatelle, however, as the aubergines become creamy, coating the egg pasta nicely.

6 tablespoons olive oil
2 large aubergines, cut into discs 1cm thick
1 garlic clove, finely sliced
400g can of chopped tomatoes
8 basil leaves, torn
a pinch of dried chilli flakes
250g fresh tagliatelle (or dried egg tagliatelle)
75g pecorino cheese, grated
sea salt and freshly ground black pepper

Heat 5 tablespoons of the oil in a large frying pan and fry the aubergines, in batches, until light golden on the outside and soft all the way through. As each batch is done, place on kitchen paper to absorb the excess oil.

Heat the remaining olive oil in a pan, add the sliced garlic and cook gently until softened. Add the tomatoes, bring to the boil and simmer until reduced by half. Season to taste. Cut the fried aubergines into strips 2cm thick and add to the tomato sauce with the basil, dried chilli and some seasoning.

Cook the tagliatelle in a large pan of boiling salted water for about 3 minutes, until *al dente* (or cook according to the packet instructions for dried tagliatelle). Drain, reserving a little of the cooking water, and add to the sauce. Toss well, adding a couple of spoonfuls of the pasta water to loosen the sauce if necessary, and cook gently for a couple of minutes. Serve with the grated pecorino and some black pepper.

Linguine with Grilled Yellow Peppers, Tomatoes, Capers, Anchovies and Marjoram

Grilling yellow peppers brings out their sweetness, even though you are charring the skin. Anchovies, capers and marjoram are the major seasonings here, while the addition of tomatoes brings everything together. It's perfect for late summer.

3 large yellow peppers
2 tablespoons olive oil
1 garlic clove, finely sliced
1 tablespoon small capers in vinegar, drained
6 salted anchovy fillets in olive oil
1 teaspoon chopped marjoram
400g can of chopped tomatoes
400g linguine
sea salt and freshly ground black pepper

Burn the skin on the yellow peppers by putting them under a hot grill or directly on a gas flame, turning them regularly until they are blackened and blistered all over. Place them in a bowl, cover with cling film and leave to cool, then take off all the blackened skin. Break each pepper in half and scrape out the seeds. Cut into strips 1cm wide.

Heat the olive oil in a large frying pan, add the garlic and cook gently until softened. Add the strips of yellow pepper and cook for 5 minutes. Add the capers, anchovies and marjoram and cook, stirring, until the anchovies have melted into the oil. Stir in the tomatoes and cook slowly for 15–20 minutes. Season to taste.

Cook the linguine in a large pan of boiling salted water until *al dente*, then drain. Add to the sauce, toss well and cook gently for a couple of minutes. Serve with a good dash of olive oil and some black pepper. Don't serve Parmesan.

Spaghetti with Aubergines, Peppers, Plum Tomatoes and Capers

This is pure sunshine, the best of seasonal summer ingredients, cooked with olive oil and seasoned with capers. Good aubergines make a deliciously creamy sauce. Always try to use very fresh, firm ones, as they generally won't have seeds in them, making the sauce sweet rather than acidic.

6 tablespoons olive oil
2 aubergines, cut lengthwise into slices 1cm thick
1 garlic clove, finely sliced
1 small onion, finely sliced
1 red and 1 yellow pepper, deseeded and cut into 1cm strips
400g can of chopped plum tomatoes
1 tablespoon capers in vinegar, drained
2 tablespoons chopped flat-leaf parsley
400g spaghetti
50g ricotta salata cheese, grated
sea salt and freshly ground black pepper

Put 4 tablespoons of the olive oil in a large, heavy-based frying pan and place over a high heat. Add the aubergine slices to the hot oil and fry for 2 minutes on each side; the aubergine is cooked when a knife inserted in the centre meets no resistance. Remove the aubergines from the pan and place on kitchen paper to absorb excess oil.

Wipe the frying pan clean, add the remaining olive oil and the garlic and cook gently until the garlic is soft but not coloured. Add the onion and cook until soft. Stir in the peppers and leave to stew gently for 10–15 minutes; this will make them sweet and slightly sticky. Add the chopped tomatoes and cook for a further 10 minutes. Cut the cooked aubergines into strips and add to the peppers and tomatoes. Finally stir in the capers and parsley. Season to taste.

Cook the spaghetti in a large pan of boiling salted water until *al dente*, then drain. Add to the sauce, toss well and cook gently for a minute or two. Serve with the grated ricotta salata.

Tagliatelle with Turnips, Lentils, Pancetta and Cream

Turnips may seem unusual in this dish but there are lots of classic Italian recipes, particularly from Puglia, where the greens from the turnips are used. This is a good dish to try if you have small, sweet turnips. Large ones tend to be too strong and would overpower the dish.

2 tablespoons olive oil
1 garlic clove, finely sliced
75g pancetta, cut into matchsticks
200g small turnips, peeled and finely sliced
100ml double cream
100g Castelluccio lentils, boiled until tender, or canned Puy lentils, drained
1 tablespoon chopped flat-leaf parsley
250g fresh tagliatelle (or dried egg tagliatelle)
100g Parmesan cheese, freshly grated
sea salt and freshly ground black pepper

Heat the olive oil in a saucepan, add the garlic and cook gently until softened. Add the pancetta and cook until it turns light golden brown. Drain off any excess fat and add the finely sliced turnips. Reduce the heat and cover the pan with a lid so the turnips steam. When they are tender enough for you to put a knife through them easily, add the double cream and cook gently for 4 minutes. Stir in the cooked lentils and the parsley, then season to taste.

Cook the tagliatelle in a large pan of boiling salted water for about 3 minutes, until *al dente* (or cook according to the packet instructions for dried tagliatelle). Drain, reserving a little of the cooking water, and toss with the turnips, lentils and pancetta. Add 2 or 3 spoonfuls of the pasta water, plus the grated Parmesan, toss well and cook gently for a couple of minutes. Serve with black pepper.

Tagliatelle with Broad Beans, Fennel Greens and Pecorino Sardo

Fennel greens and broad beans are a very popular combination in southern Italy. If you can find fennel herb, use that; otherwise the feathery tops of a fennel bulb will do. Don't use dill, however, as the flavour will be overpowering and you won't taste the broad beans.

2 tablespoons olive oil
1 garlic clove, finely sliced
1 spring onion, finely chopped
300g podded small broad beans
2 tablespoons chopped fennel greens
250g fresh tagliatelle (or dried egg tagliatelle)
100g pecorino sardo cheese, grated
sea salt and freshly ground black pepper

Heat half the olive oil in a large, heavy-based saucepan, add the garlic and spring onion and cook gently until soft. Add the broad beans, cover with water and simmer over a medium heat until almost all the water has evaporated. Season well and add the chopped fennel greens.

Cook the tagliatelle in a large pan of boiling salted water for about 3 minutes, until *al dente* (or cook according to the packet instructions for dried tagliatelle). Drain, reserving a spoonful or two of the cooking water, and add to the sauce. Toss well, adding the remaining olive oil and the reserved pasta water. Toss in half the grated cheese, then serve with the remaining cheese and some black pepper.

Ravioli with Sweet Potato, Fennel and Chilli

Sweet potatoes come in all shapes and sizes but I find the ones with bright orange flesh tend to be the nicest. They have a similar quality to squash, but with a much drier texture, which makes them suitable to use as a stuffing for ravioli.

200g sweet potatoes, peeled and cut into quarters
1 fennel bulb, cut into quarters (reserve and finely chop the feathery tops)
75g mascarpone cheese
½ quantity of Pasta Dough (see page 13)
2 tablespoons olive oil
1 red chilli, deseeded and finely chopped
sea salt and freshly ground black pepper
freshly grated Parmesan cheese, to serve

Cook the sweet potatoes and fennel in boiling salted water until soft. Drain through a colander, then leave for a few minutes so the excess moisture steams off. Put the potato and fennel through a mouli-légumes or potato ricer to make a very fine mash. Leave to cool, then mix in the mascarpone and some seasoning.

Roll out the pasta dough and make the ravioli as described on page 16. Add the ravioli to a large pan of boiling salted water and simmer for 3–5 minutes, until *al dente*. Drain and toss with the olive oil, fennel tops and chilli. Serve with grated Parmesan and some black pepper.

Rotolo di Spinaci

This classic recipe is found all over Italy. It's a wonderful dish to make in advance, as you can assemble it a few hours ahead and then bake it when you need it. The pasta is laid out on a tea towel, covered with a filling of spinach and ricotta, then rolled up, wrapped in the tea towel and poached in a large pan of water. It's very important to use a white tea towel – I once made a rotolo using a blue tea towel and the pasta came out blue, which went down very well with my friends. I still get teased about it.

1kg fresh spinach
1 garlic clove, finely sliced
50g unsalted butter
2 teaspoons chopped marjoram
500g ricotta cheese
½ quantity of Pasta Dough (see page 13)
1 quantity of Canned Tomato Sauce (see page 35)
50g Parmesan cheese, freshly grated
sea salt and freshly ground black pepper

Put the spinach in a large pan of boiling salted water, cook for 1 minute, then strain through a colander and leave to cool. Squeeze out the excess water and chop the spinach roughly.
Gently fry the garlic in the butter until softened, then remove from the heat and add the marjoram, spinach and ricotta cheese. Season with salt and pepper and leave to cool.

Roll the pasta out into 3 sheets (see page 13) and place them on a white tea towel. Using a little water and a pastry brush, join the sheets together, allowing a 1cm overlap. Spread the filling over the pasta as evenly as possible. Fold over the edge of the pasta nearest to you and, using the tea towel and the weight of the pasta, roll it away from you like you would a swiss roll. Brush the open edge of the pasta with a little water and press together to seal. Wrap the pasta roll tightly in the tea towel and tie a piece of string round it every 10cm or so, then tie the ends with string to secure them. Place the roll in a large pan of boiling water (a fish kettle is ideal) and poach for 20 minutes. Remove from the water and leave to cool.

Gently unwrap the rotolo and cut it into slices 1cm thick. Arrange them in an oval earthenware dish, cover with the tomato sauce, then sprinkle over the Parmesan cheese. Bake in an oven preheated to 190°C/Gas Mark 5 for 15 minutes.

Rigatoni with Radicchio, Pancetta and Rosemary

Rigatoni is one of my favourite pastas. I actually prefer it to penne, particularly with a creamy, meaty sauce such as this one.

4 tablespoons olive oil
1 red onion, finely chopped
1 garlic clove, finely chopped
1 teaspoon chopped rosemary
75g pancetta, cut into matchsticks
2 heads of radicchio, finely shredded
150ml double cream
juice of 1 lemon
300g rigatoni
sea salt and freshly ground black pepper
freshly grated Parmesan cheese, to serve

Heat the olive oil in a large frying pan, add the onion and garlic and cook gently for about 5 minutes, until soft. Add the rosemary and pancetta and cook for 5 minutes longer. Add the radicchio and cook for about 10 minutes, until it has wilted down. Add the lemon juice, pour in the cream and cook for 4 minutes. Season to taste.

Cook the rigatoni in a large pan of boiling salted water until *al dente*, then drain. Add to the sauce, toss well and cook gently for a couple of minutes. Serve with grated Parmesan cheese.

Cannolicchi with Zucchini and Pesto

Cannolicchi are large pasta rings. I love the way the cream in this dish brings the zucchini and pesto together, so they lightly coat the pasta.

3 medium-sized zucchini
2 tablespoons olive oil
400g cannolicchi
4 tablespoons double cream
150g Pesto (see page 207)
75g Parmesan cheese, freshly grated, plus extra to serve
8 basil leaves, torn
sea salt and freshly ground black pepper

Cut the zucchini into rounds 1cm thick, then lay them flat and cut into 1cm sticks. Heat the olive oil in a large frying pan, add the zucchini and cook gently for 5–7 minutes, until tender and slightly soft. Remove from the heat.

Add the cannolicchi to a large pan of boiling salted water and cook until *al dente*. Meanwhile, put the pan of zucchini back on the heat and add the cream. Turn the heat up full and cook for 1 minute, then season. Add the pesto and Parmesan. Drain the cooked pasta, reserving a little of the cooking water, and add it to the zucchini. Cook gently together for 2 minutes, tossing frequently. Finally add the torn basil, plus a little of the pasta cooking water if necessary. The pasta should be quite juicy, with a nice coating of sauce. Serve with black pepper and more Parmesan if required.

Penne with Broad Beans, Mint and Coppa di Parma

Italian broad beans are available in the UK from February but the best time to make this dish is when British beans are in season, from late April/May. Always try to use small broad beans, as they have an amazing sweet flavour and a lovely texture. If you really have to use large ones, blanch them first and take off the thick, indigestible skin. Frozen broad beans tend to lack flavour and are not as successful as frozen peas, so stick to fresh.

2 tablespoons olive oil
2 spring onions, finely chopped
350g podded small broad beans
200ml water
8 slices of coppa di Parma, cut into strips 1cm thick
1 teaspoon chopped mint
1 tablespoon mascarpone cheese
400g penne rigate
sea salt and freshly ground black pepper
freshly grated Parmesan cheese, to serve

Heat the olive oil in a pan, add the spring onions and cook gently for 5–7 minutes, until softened. Add the broad beans and cook for a couple of minutes, then add the water and simmer until it has completely evaporated. Stir in the coppa di Parma, mint and finally the mascarpone. Check the seasoning.

Cook the penne in a large pan of boiling salted water until *al dente*, then drain, reserving a spoonful or two of the cooking water. Add the pasta to the broad beans and toss well together. Season, add the reserved cooking water to make the pasta juicy, then cook gently for a couple of minutes. Serve with grated Parmesan and some black pepper.

Taglierini with Peas, Prosciutto and Parmesan

I first ate this in a little restaurant called the Grotto di Cornigans, which is in the middle of nowhere but very much in the heart of the Valpolicella wine district. It's a spring pasta dish, using the tiny first peas, which are available from April in Italy. Fresh peas have a very short season but you could use good-quality frozen peas, making this dish available all year round.

1 small spring onion, finely sliced
50g unsalted butter
200g shelled young fresh peas
150g prosciutto, sliced
250g fresh taglierini (or dried egg taglierini)
50g Parmesan cheese, freshly grated
sea salt and freshly ground black pepper

Sweat the spring onion in the butter until soft, then add the peas and a dash of water. Cook for 5 minutes or until the peas are tender. Stir in the prosciutto.

Cook the taglierini in a large pan of boiling salted water for about 3 minutes, until *al dente* (or cook according to the packet instructions for dried taglierini). Drain, reserving a few spoonfuls of the cooking water, and add to the peas and prosciutto. Toss together, adding a little of the reserved cooking water to loosen the sauce if necessary. Cook over a low heat for 2 minutes, then add the grated Parmesan, season and serve.

Penne with Zucchini and Prosciutto

This is another easy pasta sauce. The addition of prosciutto gives it a real boost, as zucchini can be quite subtle on their own.

4 medium-sized zucchini
I tablespoon olive oil
I garlic clove, finely sliced
I teaspoon chopped mint
6 slices of prosciutto di Parma, cut into strips
100ml double cream
400g penne rigate
75g Parmesan cheese, freshly grated
sea salt and freshly ground black pepper

Trim the ends off the zucchini, then cut them in half lengthways. Lay them flat-side down and cut into half moons about 1cm thick.

Heat the olive oil in a large frying pan, add the garlic and cook until softened. Add the zucchini and cook gently for 10–15 minutes, until they are soft and have stuck slightly to the bottom of the pan. Add the mint, prosciutto strips and finally the double cream. Season well.

Cook the penne in a large pan of boiling salted water until *al dente*, then drain, reserving a little of the cooking water. Add the pasta to the sauce, toss well and add a few tablespoons of the pasta water to thin it out. Cook over a low heat for a couple of minutes, then add the Parmesan, toss again and serve with black pepper.

Tagliatelle with Artichokes, Asparagus and Thyme

As you've probably figured out if you've looked through this book, the artichoke is my favourite vegetable. Here, artichokes and asparagus make an unusual combination but their textures are similar and their flavours actually complement each other.

The only problem with this dish is what to drink with it, as anyone who knows about wine will tell you that artichokes and asparagus always pose a challenge.

4 artichokes
250g asparagus
1 tablespoon olive oil
1 garlic clove, finely sliced
1 teaspoon chopped thyme
100ml double cream
250g fresh tagliatelle (or dried egg tagliatelle)
100g Parmesan cheese, freshly grated
sea salt and freshly ground black pepper

Cook the artichokes whole in a pan of boiling water until you can put a knife easily through the heart. Drain and leave to cool, then remove the leaves and any dark green parts. Cut 3cm off the top of each artichoke, scoop out the choke, then slice the artichokes 1cm thick.

Cook the asparagus in boiling salted water until tender, then drain. Cut it into 1cm rounds. Heat the olive oil in a large frying pan, add the garlic and cook gently until soft. Add the thyme, asparagus and artichokes, season, then add the double cream and cook for 4 minutes.

Cook the tagliatelle in a large pan of boiling salted water for about 3 minutes, until *al dente* (or cook according to the packet instructions for dried tagliatelle). Drain, reserving a little of the cooking water, and add to the asparagus and artichoke sauce. Toss well, adding the Parmesan and one or two spoonfuls of the pasta cooking water. Serve with black pepper.

Tortellini with Artichokes, Onion Squash and Fontina Cheese

The inspiration for this came from a restaurant I visited in Piedmont. The mixture of artichoke and onion squash, boiled and turned into a filling, had a very interesting flavour, particularly with the addition of the fontina. Happily, the restaurant served it with ridiculous amounts of white truffle. I highly recommend it with or without the truffle, but do try it with if you get the opportunity. If you can get hold of them, you could use black summer truffles, as they are more affordable and easier to obtain. They seem to be flourishing in the British climate.

4 artichokes
1 small onion squash, peeled, deseeded and chopped
150g unsalted butter
1 garlic clove, finely sliced
1 teaspoon chopped thyme
100g fontina cheese, grated
½ quantity of Pasta Dough (see page 13)
25g white truffle (optional)
sea salt and freshly ground black pepper

Cook the artichokes whole in a pan of boiling water until you can put a knife easily through the heart. Drain and leave to cool, then remove the leaves and any dark green parts. Cut 3cm off the top of each artichoke, scoop out the choke and chop the artichokes into a fine mince.

Cook the onion squash in boiling salted water until very tender, then drain and set aside.
Melt half the butter in a large frying pan, add the garlic and cook gently until soft. Add the thyme, artichokes and onion squash and cook, stirring with a wooden spoon, until the onion squash has turned into a mash. Season, add the fontina cheese and leave to cool.

Roll out the pasta dough as thinly as your pasta machine will let you (see page 13). Using a pastry cutter, cut out 8cm rounds and place a teaspoonful of the mixture on each one. Brush the edges of each round with water, then fold in half so you have a half-moon shape. Bring the 2 corners up towards you, overlap them and squeeze tight. You have made your first tortellino. Repeat this process until you have used up all the filling. The tortellini can be kept in the fridge on a floured tray for up to 2 days or can be cooked straight away.

Cook the tortellini in a large pan of boiling salted water for 3–5 minutes, until *al dente*. Meanwhile, soften the remaining butter in a large frying pan, but don't let it melt completely. Drain the pasta and toss with the butter. Shave over the white truffle, if using, and serve with black pepper.

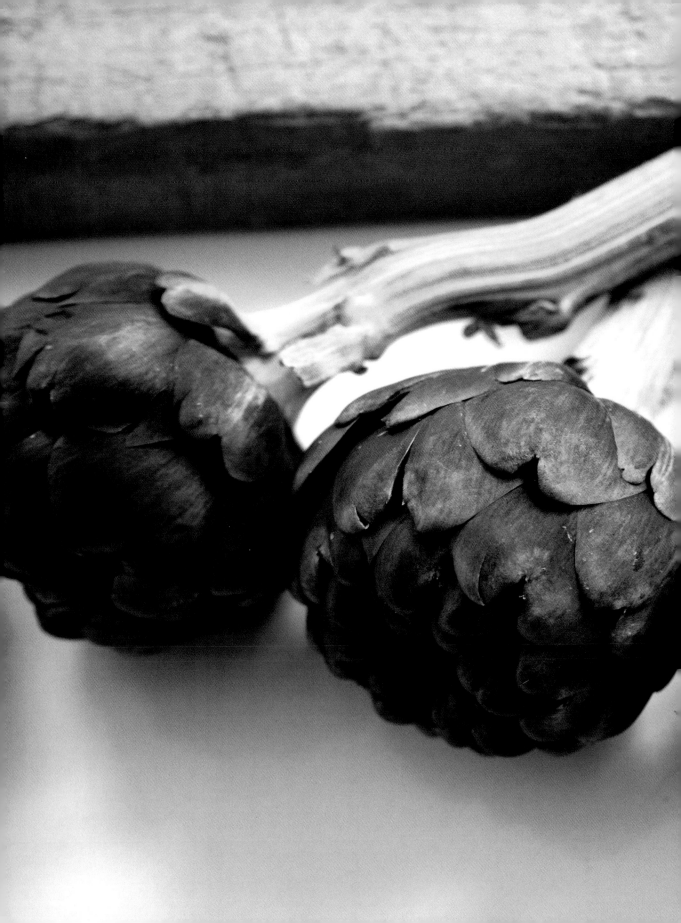

Gnocchi with Butternut Squash, Pancetta, Thyme and Mascarpone

This is comfort food at its best. Butternut squash is the easiest and probably the most consistent squash to buy, but feel free to experiment with a crown prince or an onion squash instead.

1 medium butternut squash, peeled, deseeded and cut into cubes
1 tablespoon olive oil
1 garlic clove, finely sliced
75g sliced pancetta
1 teaspoon chopped thyme
2 tablespoons mascarpone cheese
500g potato gnocchi (see page 18)
75g Parmesan cheese, freshly grated, plus extra to serve
sea salt and freshly ground black pepper

Cook the butternut squash cubes in boiling salted water until very tender, then drain and set aside. Heat the olive oil in a large frying pan, add the garlic and cook gently until soft. Add the pancetta and thyme and cook until the pancetta is lightly golden. Add the cooked butternut squash and use a wooden spoon to mash it together with the pancetta and garlic. Stir in the mascarpone and cook slowly for about 5 minutes, until you have a creamy butternut squash mash.

Add the gnocchi to a large pan of boiling salted water and cook for 2–3 minutes, until they rise to the top of the pan. Remove with a slotted spoon and add to the sauce. Thin the sauce with a little of the gnocchi cooking water, then add the Parmesan and some black pepper and toss well. Check the seasoning and serve in hot bowls, with a little Parmesan on top.

Gnocchi with Zucchini and their Flowers, Basil, Cream and Parmesan

If you are lucky enough to have zucchini growing in your garden, this is the dish to try. If not, the zucchini flowers don't really add a huge amount of flavour – they're more for colour and texture – so you can make it without them.

8 medium-sized zucchini, with their flowers
1 tablespoon olive oil
1 garlic clove, finely sliced
8 basil leaves, torn
100ml double cream
500g potato gnocchi (see page 18)
100g Parmesan cheese, freshly grated
sea salt and freshly ground black pepper

Remove the flowers from the zucchini and cut off the bottom of each flower to take out the bitter stamen. Cut the zucchini lengthways in half and then cut into half moons about 5mm thick. Rip the flowers into strips and set aside.

Heat the olive oil in a large saucepan, add the garlic and cook gently until softened. Add the sliced zucchini, turn down the heat to its lowest setting and cover the pan. Cook the zucchini for about 8 minutes until just tender, then season. Add the basil and zucchini flowers, then the double cream, and cook, uncovered for 4–5 minutes.

Add the gnocchi to a large pan of boiling salted water and cook for 2–3 minutes, until they rise to the top of the pan. Remove with a slotted spoon, and add to the sauce. Add the Parmesan and a spoonful or two of the gnocchi cooking liquid, toss together and serve with black pepper.

Gnocchi with Spinach, Crème Fraîche, Chilli and Pancetta

Even though it's quite easy to make gnocchi (see page 18), it's a bit time consuming if you want a quick dinner, so I often use the De Cecco brand, which is very good quality. This dish is very satisfying to make and also to eat, with its lovely bright colours and a richness that makes the gnocchi taste even better.

600g fresh spinach
1 tablespoon olive oil
1 garlic clove, finely sliced
100g pancetta, cut into matchsticks
1 red chilli, deseeded and finely chopped
100ml crème fraîche
100g Parmesan cheese, freshly grated
500g potato gnocchi
sea salt and freshly ground black pepper

Put the spinach in a large pan of boiling salted water and cook for 1 minute, then strain through a colander. Leave to cool, then squeeze out the excess water. Chop the spinach finely.

Heat the olive oil in a large pan, add the garlic and pancetta and cook until light golden. Drain off any excess fat, then add the red chilli and the chopped spinach. Season and stir in the crème fraîche and Parmesan.

Add the gnocchi to a large pan of boiling salted water and cook for 2–3 minutes, until they rise to the top of the pan. Remove with a slotted spoon and add to the sauce. Toss well and add a spoonful or two of the gnocchi cooking water if needed. Toss again and serve with black pepper.

Ravioli with Dried Broad Beans and Braised Cicoria

I had the idea for this during a summer holiday in Puglia, where every restaurant had on its menu an antipasti of dried broad beans cooked to a purée and served with bitter, earthy braised cicoria, dressed with really top-quality Puglian olive oil. I've used the broad bean purée as a stuffing for ravioli here and served it tossed with the braised cicoria. If you can't get hold of cicoria, you could use wild dandelions in spring.

200g dried skinless broad beans
1 small potato, peeled
1 fresh red chilli
100ml good olive oil
200g cicoria, tough larger stems removed
1 tablespoon olive oil
1 garlic clove, finely sliced
1 dried red chilli
½ quantity of Pasta Dough (see page 13)
sea salt and freshly ground black pepper

Put the dried broad beans in a saucepan, add enough cold water to cover them by 5cm, then add the whole peeled potato and the whole fresh chilli. Bring to the boil, reduce the heat and simmer for 45 minutes–1 hour, until the beans are very soft. Drain off the cooking liquid but keep a little back. Put the beans, potato and chilli through a fine mouli-légumes (or crush them with a potato masher). Season, then stir in the 100ml olive oil, plus a little of the cooking water if the mixture appears to be too dry; it should have the consistency of creamy mashed potato.

Cook the cicoria in a pan of boiling salted water until the stems are tender. This may take 10 minutes, because cicoria is quite tough and it can be very bitter if you don't cook it for long enough. Drain the cicoria and chop roughly. Heat the olive oil in a frying pan, add the garlic and cook gently until softened. Add the blanched cicoria and dried chilli and cook for 2–3 minutes. Season to taste and set aside.

Roll out the pasta dough and make the ravioli as described on page 16. Add the ravioli to a large pan of boiling salted water and simmer for 3–5 minutes, until *al dente*. Meanwhile put the cicoria back on the heat. Drain the ravioli and toss with the braised cicoria. Serve with a dash of good olive oil and some black pepper. No Parmesan.

Fungi

Fungi

Mushrooms and truffles are highly prized in Italian cooking, with truffles being the most sought-after ingredient of all. There is nothing better than really well-made taglierini tossed in butter and finished with a generous grating of fresh white truffle.

The most significant mushroom in culinary terms is the porcini, known as the cep in France and the penny bun in the UK. If you ever pick your own porcini and are lucky enough to find too many, they're very easy to dry. Just string good slices of mushroom on to cotton thread and hang them somewhere cool and dry for about a week.

Portobello mushrooms are currently quite fashionable and are very easy to get hold of. They are essentially flat field mushrooms with a fairly strong flavour. When cooked slowly with olive oil, garlic and parsley, they can taste almost like steak. With the addition of some dried porcini, they make the most wonderful simple pasta sauce (see page 95).

Mushroom nomenclature can occasionally be confusing. The mushroom that used to be known as a chanterelle is now commonly called a girolle. This is a French term but is widely used in markets all over the UK and in restaurants. The French use the word chanterelle to describe two varieties: the chanterelle gris, or grey chanterelle, and the chanterelle jaune, which is yellow. The most important fact about these mushrooms is that they all come from the chanterelle family, and are interchangeable in recipes. The magical thing about chanterelles is the perfume that they give off. It is one mushroom you can wash without affecting its flavour too much.

Truffles are not really mushrooms at all – the simplest way to describe them is as the fruit of a fungus. They grow underground, so are very difficult to spot. In Italy, dogs are used to find the prized white truffle, pigs for the black one. As there is so much money involved – white truffles are currently going for up to £3,000 per kilo – the competition is very high and can be quite unpleasant. There are many tricks to increase the weight of a truffle, so when buying one check that it doesn't have mud in any holes or crevices, otherwise that is what you will be paying for.

If you want to buy a fresh truffle, try a good Italian delicatessen – you can pretty much guarantee that an Italian will not last a year without a taste of a white truffle. They are in season from early October to December, or when the first hard frost arrives. They have become incredibly popular over the last few years, causing the price to increase dramatically. But there is nothing quite as exciting as the smell of fresh white truffles. They have a unique flavour that needs very little help.

There are many types of black truffle, the most famous being the Périgord, which grows not just in France but also in Italy. Generally available from November to February, it has a very distinctive taste, quite unlike the white truffle, and is absolutely delicious with pasta and cream – try Taglierini with Black Truffle, Artichokes and Cream on page 101.

The summer truffle, available from spring and throughout the summer, is affordable as far as truffles go – but beware: just because it's a truffle doesn't necessarily mean it will have masses of flavour.

Pennette with Chanterelles, Parsley and Mascarpone

My kids love pennette because it's so small – it's pretty much a third of the size of regular penne. What's particularly good about this dish is that when the mushrooms are cooked down, they amalgamate with the small pasta, giving a nice ratio of pasta to mushroom in every mouthful.

The best chanterelles come from Scotland. They have a lovely apricot colour and aroma and are grown in a more humid atmosphere than chanterelles from other parts of Europe – which during the summer can be quite dry and flavourless. The higher water content of Scottish chanterelles makes them generally more flavoursome. In this recipe, I've shown a way of effectively blanching the mushrooms in their own juices to concentrate the flavour and reduce any unwanted moisture, which can translate on the plate to being slimy.

2 tablespoons olive oil
500g chanterelle mushrooms, trimmed
1 garlic clove, finely sliced
a pinch of dried chilli flakes
2 tablespoons chopped flat-leaf parsley
3 tablespoons mascarpone cheese
½ lemon
400g pennette
sea salt and freshly ground black pepper
freshly grated Parmesan cheese, to serve

Heat half the olive oil in a large frying pan, add the mushrooms and cook over a high heat for 3 minutes, so they release their water. Drain the mushrooms, discarding the liquid. Wipe the pan clean, add the remaining oil and the garlic and chilli and cook until the garlic is soft. Add the parsley and cooked chanterelles and cook over a low heat for 4–5 minutes. Stir in the mascarpone and a squeeze of lemon, then season with salt and pepper.

Cook the pennette in a large pan of boiling salted water until *al dente*, then drain, reserving a spoonful or two of the cooking water. Add the pasta to the mushrooms, mix together and stir in a little of the cooking water to loosen the sauce, if necessary. Cook over a low heat for 2 minutes, then serve with grated Parmesan and black pepper.

Tagliatelle with Dried Porcini, Zucchini and Mint

In Italian cooking, dried porcini tend to be used as a seasoning rather than a main ingredient. A kilo of fresh porcini is needed to make 100g dried ones, so even though they seem expensive a little goes a very long way.

Always buy dried porcini you can see in the packet, so you can check that the pieces aren't broken and they are not too dark – the darker they are, generally the older they are. When the mushrooms become very dark, the flavour after soaking is extremely strong, almost like Marmite, and can overpower everything else.

75g dried porcini mushrooms
2 tablespoons olive oil
2 garlic cloves, finely sliced
200g zucchini, sliced into fine discs
2 tablespoons mascarpone cheese
2 teaspoons chopped mint
250g fresh tagliatelle (or dried egg tagliatelle)
sea salt and freshly ground black pepper
freshly grated Parmesan cheese, to serve

Place the porcini in a bowl and pour over enough boiling water to cover. Leave to cool, then remove the softened mushrooms and strain the liquid through a fine sieve.

Heat a tablespoon of the olive oil in a large saucepan, add half the garlic and cook gently until softened. Add the mushrooms and cook for 2 minutes. Add the strained soaking liquor and simmer until it reduces to a syrup. Remove the mushrooms and their cooking juices from the pan and keep to one side.

Heat the remaining olive oil in the pan, add the remaining garlic and cook gently until soft but not brown. Add the zucchini, raise the heat and cook until they are tender and lightly coloured. Return the porcini and their juices to the pan, season, then stir in the mascarpone and mint.

Cook the tagliatelle in a large pan of boiling salted water for about 3 minutes, until *al dente* (or cook according to the packet instructions for dried tagliatelle). Drain, reserving a few spoonfuls of the cooking water, and toss the pasta with the porcini and zucchini sauce. Add a little of the reserved cooking water if necessary to loosen the sauce. Cook gently for a couple of minutes, then serve with black pepper and grated Parmesan.

Gnocchi with Jerusalem Artichokes, White Truffle, Cream and Parmesan

The Jerusalem artichoke is a tuber not unlike a potato but with a slightly crisper texture and an earthy flavour. With the addition of double cream and Parmesan, it becomes surprisingly luxurious. The flavour is released into the cream, making it perfect for coating gnocchi. If you can manage to treat yourself to a truffle, it will make this dish even more special.

250g peeled Jerusalem artichokes (you will need roughly 500g unpeeled artichokes), finely sliced
150ml double cream
½ garlic clove, finely sliced
100g Parmesan cheese, freshly grated
500g potato gnocchi (see page 18)
25g fresh white truffle
sea salt and freshly ground black pepper

Cook the Jerusalem artichokes in a pan of boiling salted water until they are tender but still have a little bite left to them. Drain and set aside.

In a small frying pan or sauté pan, boil the cream with the sliced garlic for 5 minutes. Add the Jerusalem artichokes and Parmesan cheese and season to taste. Remove from the heat.

Add the gnocchi to a large pan of boiling salted water and cook for 2–3 minutes, until they rise to the top of the pan. Remove with a slotted spoon, drain and combine with the artichoke mixture. Toss well, adding a spoonful or two of the gnocchi cooking water to loosen the sauce if required. Place in wide pasta bowls and finely grate over the white truffle.

Tagliatelle with Porcini, Tomatoes and Cream

I recommend keeping a little jar of dried porcini mushrooms sitting in the back of your cupboard. They are a very versatile seasoning and are especially delicious with a basic tomato sauce and a dash of cream.

When you add the cream to this dish, it's best to let it cook without stirring it in, otherwise the sauce becomes emulsified and too creamy. If you don't stir it, not only does it taste better but you also get a lovely, rippled effect of cooked cream and bright red tomato sauce.

2 tablespoons olive oil
2 garlic cloves, finely sliced
50g dried porcini mushrooms, soaked in 100ml hot water for 10 minutes
400g can of chopped tomatoes
5 tablespoons double cream
2 tablespoons chopped flat-leaf parsley
250g fresh tagliatelle (or dried egg tagliatelle)
sea salt and freshly ground black pepper
freshly grated Parmesan cheese, to serve

Heat the olive oil in a large, heavy-based saucepan or frying pan, add the garlic and cook gently for 1 minute, until softened. Drain the soaked mushrooms, reserving the liquid. Add the mushrooms to the pan and then gradually add half the soaking water. Cook for 10 minutes or until the mushrooms are soft; the liquid should have reduced to a syrupy consistency. Add the tomatoes and cook slowly for 20 minutes, until the sauce is reduced and thickened. Add the double cream but don't stir. Let the cream cook into the sauce for 3–5 minutes, then add the chopped parsley and season to taste. At this point you'll have to stir the sauce a little but try not to do it too much.

Cook the tagliatelle in a large pan of boiling salted water for about 3 minutes, until *al dente* (or cook according to the packet instructions for dried tagliatelle). Drain and add to the sauce. Toss well, cook over a low heat for 1 minute, then serve with grated Parmesan and black pepper.

Rigatoni with Portobello and Porcini Mushrooms

This is one of my favourite autumn dishes. Portobello mushrooms have an amazing amount of flavour, which becomes very concentrated if you cook them for a long time. With the addition of dried porcini, it becomes a really full-on mushroom experience. Rigatoni is the best pasta for this, as it seems to absorb the flavour of the mushrooms and the ridges hold on to the pieces.

3 tablespoons olive oil
2 garlic cloves, finely sliced
2 tablespoons chopped thyme
250g portobello mushrooms, cut into slices 5mm thick
50g dried porcini mushrooms, soaked in 100ml hot water for 10 minutes
100ml double cream
½ lemon
400g rigatoni
sea salt and freshly ground black pepper
freshly grated Parmesan cheese, to serve

Heat the olive oil in a large frying pan, add the garlic and thyme and cook for a couple of minutes, until soft. Add the portobello mushrooms and cook slowly for about 15 minutes. The mushrooms will lose a lot of water and will boil slightly for a minute or two. Keep on cooking until all the water has been absorbed back into the mushrooms.

Drain the soaked porcini mushrooms, reserving the cooking water, and chop them. Add them to the pan with half their soaking water and cook for about 10 minutes, until the mushrooms look juicy but not wet. Add the double cream and a squeeze of lemon, season and cook for 2 minutes longer.

Cook the rigatoni in a large pan of boiling salted water until *al dente*, then drain, reserving a spoonful or two of the cooking water. Add the pasta to the sauce, together with a little of the cooking water to loosen it if necessary. Toss well and cook over a low heat for 2 minutes. Adjust the seasoning and serve with grated Parmesan.

Stracci with Trompettes de la Mort

Trompette de la mort is a rather unfortunate name for such a delicious mushroom. It means trumpet of death, and they are probably so called because they are dark and look rather evil. The English name is horn of plenty, which is considerably more appealing. Their flavour is quite earthy but the most amazing thing is their texture, which is chewy but always very juicy.

When you add the double cream to this dish, the sauce changes colour to a dark grey. With the addition of flat-leaf parsley and the rough-looking pasta, it's extremely appetising.

½ quantity of Pasta Dough (see page 13)
2 tablespoons olive oil
300g trompettes de la mort mushrooms, stems removed
1 garlic clove, finely sliced
1 tablespoon chopped flat-leaf parsley
½ lemon
100ml double cream
sea salt and freshly ground black pepper
freshly grated Parmesan cheese, to serve

To make stracci, all you need to do is roll out the pasta into 60cm × 12cm sheets (see page 13) and cut it into 6cm triangles; they don't have to be perfect, as stracci means 'ripped'.

Heat half the oil in a large frying pan, add the mushrooms and cook over a high heat for 2–3 minutes. All the water should come out and start to boil. At this point, drain the mushrooms through a colander, discarding the water. Wipe clean the frying pan, add the remaining olive oil and gently cook the garlic in it until soft. Return the mushrooms to the pan with the chopped parsley, a squeeze of lemon and finally the double cream. Leave to cook for about 5 minutes on a low heat. The cream will turn a luxurious grey-black colour. Season to taste.

Cook the stracci in a large pan of boiling salted water for 3 minutes or until *al dente*. Drain, reserving a little of the cooking water, and add to the mushroom sauce. Add a little of the reserved water if necessary to loosen the sauce, then cook over a low heat for 2 minutes. Serve with plenty of grated Parmesan and black pepper.

Tagliatelle with Girolles

The hardest part of this dish is probably finding the girolles. The way you cook them is very important – if you don't drain the juices off, they can be quite watery, making it a rather wet pasta.

250g fresh girolle mushrooms
1 tablespoon olive oil
75g unsalted butter
1 garlic clove, finely sliced
1 tablespoon chopped flat-leaf parsley
250g fresh tagliatelle (or dried egg tagliatelle)
sea salt and freshly ground black pepper
freshly grated Parmesan cheese, to serve

Wash the girolles in cold water and remove any muddy or sandy bits. If the mushrooms are large, cut them in half lengthways. Heat the olive oil in a large frying pan. When it is really hot, add the girolles and cook for about 2 minutes or until lots of water has come out. Drain, discarding the water, and set the mushrooms aside. Wipe the pan clean and add the butter and garlic. Cook gently until the garlic has softened, then add the cooked girolles, chopped parsley and some salt and pepper to taste.

Cook the tagliatelle in a large pan of boiling salted water for about 3 minutes, until *al dente* (or cook according to the packet instructions for dried tagliatelle). Drain, reserving a few spoonfuls of the cooking water, and add to the sauce. Adjust the seasoning, add a little of the pasta water to loosen the sauce if necessary, then toss together and cook gently for 2 minutes. Serve with grated Parmesan and plenty of black pepper.

Taglierini with Black Truffle, Artichokes and Cream

This recipe came from a restaurant in Rome and is probably the best way to eat a black truffle, as the flavour really comes out in the cream. Depending on your budget, you could also use a summer truffle.

5 small artichokes
juice of 1 lemon
2 tablespoons olive oil
1 garlic clove, finely sliced
2 tablespoons chopped flat-leaf parsley
75ml double cream
250g fresh taglierini (or dried egg taglierini)
75g fresh black or summer truffle
sea salt and freshly ground black pepper
freshly grated Parmesan cheese, to serve

Prepare the artichokes as described on page 45, slicing them thinly after soaking them in water acidulated with the lemon juice.

Heat the olive oil in a saucepan, add the garlic and cook gently for a minute or so. Stir in the artichokes, cover the pan and cook for 8–10 minutes, until tender. Add the parsley and cream and bring to the boil. Turn off the heat and season to taste.

Cook the taglierini in a large pan of boiling salted water for about 3 minutes, until *al dente* (or cook according to the packet instructions for dried taglierini). Drain, reserving a few spoonfuls of the cooking water, and add to the sauce. Toss together, adding a little of the cooking water if necessary to loosen the sauce, then cook gently for 2 minutes. Finish by grating the truffle all over the pasta. Serve with grated Parmesan and black pepper.

Tagliatelle with Black Truffle, Spinach and Cream

The combination of cream, truffle and egg yolks is undeniably rich but the spinach adds lightness and a fresh, earthy flavour.

500g fresh spinach
150ml double cream
½ garlic clove, finely sliced
4 organic egg yolks
250g fresh tagliatelle (or dried egg tagliatelle)
50g fresh winter black truffle
75g Parmesan cheese, freshly grated
sea salt and freshly ground black pepper

Put the spinach in a large pan of boiling salted water and cook for about a minute, until the stems are tender; don't overcook it, as spinach tends to lose its flavour when it is cooked for too long. Drain through a colander and leave to cool. Don't place it in iced or cold water, as all this does is dilute the flavour. Gently squeeze out most of the water, then finely chop the spinach.

In a large frying pan, bring the cream to the boil, add the sliced garlic and cook for 2 minutes. Meanwhile, beat the egg yolks together until liquid. Remove the cream from the heat, add the egg yolks and then the chopped spinach, mixing together to form a sauce.

Cook the tagliatelle in a large pan of boiling salted water for about 3 minutes, until *al dente* (or cook according to the packet instructions for dried tagliatelle). Drain, reserving a little of the cooking water, add the pasta to the sauce and toss well. With a fine grater, grate in the truffle and then add the Parmesan cheese. You will probably need to add a spoonful or two of the pasta water at this point. Toss again, adjust the seasoning if necessary and finish with any remaining truffle on top of the pasta.

Ravioli with Portobello Mushrooms, Porcini, Ricotta and Sage

This is a really tasty vegetarian ravioli, which any meat-eater would also absolutely adore (N.B. vegetarians need to use rennet-free Parmesan). Portobello mushrooms have masses of flavour if they are cooked correctly.

3 tablespoons olive oil
1 garlic clove, finely sliced
250g portobello mushrooms, sliced 1cm thick
1 teaspoon chopped thyme
50g dried porcini mushrooms, soaked in 100ml hot water for 10 minutes
200g ricotta cheese
75g Parmesan cheese, freshly grated, plus extra to serve
½ quantity of Pasta Dough (see page 13)
75g unsalted butter
6 sage leaves
sea salt and freshly ground black pepper

Heat the olive oil in a frying pan, add the garlic and cook gently until softened. Add the portobello mushrooms and thyme and cook for about 15 minutes, until all the liquid from the mushrooms has evaporated. Drain the soaked porcini, reserving the soaking water, then add the porcini and half the water to the pan. Cook until all the liquid has evaporated again; this intensifies the flavour. Remove from the heat and leave to cool. Finely chop the mushrooms, put them in a bowl and add the ricotta and Parmesan. Mix well and season to taste.

Roll out the pasta dough and make the ravioli as described on page 16. Add the ravioli to a large pan of boiling salted water and simmer for 3–5 minutes, until *al dente*. Meanwhile, soften the butter in a frying pan with the sage but don't let it melt completely. Drain the ravioli and toss with the butter and sage. Serve with black pepper and grated Parmesan.

Ravioli with Potato and White Truffle

If you are lucky enough to be able to buy a white truffle, and have three friends who are desperate to try it, this is the dish to make. The truffle is sliced and put on top of the filling, then encased in the pasta, giving it maximum flavour without losing any of the aroma.

300g floury white potatoes, such as Maris Piper, peeled
125g unsalted butter
150g Parmesan cheese, freshly grated, plus extra to serve
50ml full-fat milk
½ quantity of Pasta Dough (see page 13)
25g fresh white truffle
sea salt and freshly ground black pepper

Cook the potatoes in boiling salted water until tender, then drain through a colander. Leave in the colander for a few minutes to allow excess moisture to steam off, then pass the potatoes through a mouli-légumes or potato ricer so they are very smooth. Add 75g of the butter, plus the Parmesan, milk and some seasoning and beat with a wooden spoon until smooth.

Roll out the pasta dough and make the ravioli as described on page 16 – but before you fold the pasta over the filling, thinly slice the truffle, using a truffle slicer if you have one, on to each portion of filling (one slice per portion is enough).

Add the ravioli to a large pan of boiling salted water and simmer for 3–5 minutes, until *al dente*. Meanwhile, soften the remaining butter in a large frying pan, but don't let it melt completely. Drain the pasta and toss with the butter. Serve immediately, with some grated Parmesan and black pepper.

Fish

Fish

Fresh fish isn't necessarily the first partner you think of for pasta, but with the addition of ingredients such as zucchini or tomatoes it becomes part of the seasoning and texture of the dish rather than the main ingredient. All the recipes in this chapter are prepared using olive oil rather than butter or cream, making them particularly light and healthy.

I am very fond of sardines with pasta, especially with linguine. Sardines are easy to get hold of and, since they are an oily fish, they have lots and lots of flavour. The only downside is that you might find a few bones. Squid is another natural choice with pasta. It is almost a fish but tastes more like shellfish. When cooked at a high temperature and slightly caramelised, it releases an incredibly sweet flavour. It is important to choose small squid, as they tend to get quite tough when they are over about 300g in weight. This applies to cuttlefish too. Cuttlefish is tougher than squid but the simple rule is to cut it into very fine strips before cooking.

Various forms of preserved fish are famous for their role in pasta sauces, such as anchovies and bottarga. Bottarga, a great Sardinian delicacy, is grey mullet roe that has been salted and dried. It forms the basis of one of the all-time-classic pasta dishes, spaghetti with bottarga. I have included a variation on this using agretti, or monk's beard (see page 113). Anchovies are a staple of pasta cookery. One of the simplest and easiest sauces is spaghetti with anchovies, chilli and garlic, which is exactly what it says it is. If you are lucky enough to have some good-quality salted anchovies in oil, it makes this a real delight of a dish. Salted anchovies are widely used in this book, so it's worth investing in a decent Kilner jar of them and keeping them in the fridge. They will last at least a year.

I don't want to be bossy but it's never a great idea to add cheese to fish pasta dishes. There may be a few exceptions with cream, but it's not a great combination.

Linguine with Sardines

This is an all-time classic, and probably the best way to cook sardines apart from simply grilling them. I've had so many variations on this pasta, from Puglia to Palermo, but they're all the same basic idea.

1 fennel bulb, sliced
2 tablespoons olive oil
1 garlic clove, finely sliced
½ teaspoon fennel seeds, crushed
1 small dried red chilli, crumbled
200g sardine fillets – check for any bones
1 teaspoon raisins
100ml dry white wine
400g linguine
½ lemon
1 tablespoon chopped flat-leaf parsley
sea salt and freshly ground black pepper

Blanch the fennel in boiling salted water for a couple of minutes, then drain. Heat the olive oil in a large frying pan, add the garlic, fennel seeds and dried chilli and cook until the garlic is soft. Add the blanched fennel, then carefully place the sardine fillets in the pan so they are sitting on the other ingredients. Sprinkle over the raisins, pour in the white wine, season with salt and pepper, then cover the pan with a lid or a piece of foil. Cook over a low heat for 10–12 minutes, then check whether the sardines are done; the wine should have steamed the sardines and together they made a lovely juice.

Cook the linguine in a large pan of boiling salted water until *al dente*, then drain, reserving a few spoonfuls of the cooking water. Add the pasta to the sardines, toss well and add a little of the reserved water to loosen the sauce if necessary. Cook gently for 2 minutes. Don't worry if the sardines break up; the most important thing is that the pasta absorbs the cooking juices. Finish with a squeeze of lemon, the chopped parsley and some black pepper.

Spaghetti with Grey Mullet, Bottarga and Sea Kale

Wild sea kale is the most delicious thing if you can get it. If you can't, there is a cultivated variety, which has no resemblance whatsoever to wild sea kale in looks but has the same distinctive, minerally flavour. Alternatively, you could substitute curly kale. It won't be the same but it tastes similar.

Grey mullet is the mother of bottarga (mullet roe), so this combination of grey mullet, bottarga and sea kale is very much a family affair, and tastes pretty good too.

500g sea kale
3 tablespoons olive oil
1 garlic clove, sliced
200g grey mullet fillet, skinned and cut into 1cm slices
400g spaghetti
50g bottarga, grated
sea salt and freshly ground black pepper

Cook the sea kale in a large pan of boiling salted water until the stems are tender to the point of a knife. Drain and leave to cool, then chop roughly and set aside.

Heat the olive oil in a large frying pan, add the garlic and cook gently until soft. Stir in the sea kale, then scatter the grey mullet strips on top. Place a lid on the pan and gently steam the grey mullet for 3–4 minutes. Season to taste.

Cook the spaghetti in a large pan of boiling salted water until *al dente*. Drain, reserving a little of the cooking water, and toss the pasta with the sea kale and grey mullet. Add a spoonful or two of the pasta cooking water and cook gently over a low heat for a couple of minutes. Season with salt and pepper and serve in shallow bowls, with the grated bottarga on top. Add a dash of olive oil, perhaps, and some black pepper.

Spaghettini with Bottarga and Agretti

Agretti, or monk's beard, is the first shoots of the salsify plant. It has a very earthy flavour but the texture is the best thing. Mixed with salty, fishy bottarga (dried grey mullet roe) and spaghetti, it really lifts this classic combination. It can be hard to find in shops but funnily enough it grows wild in fields in the UK. You can buy the seeds from Franchi, which is probably the best Italian seed importer.

Bottarga is readily available in any good delicatessen, particularly a Sardinian one, or you can order it online (see www.natoora.co.uk).

3 tablespoons olive oil
3 tablespoons water
50g bottarga, grated
400g spaghettini
75g agretti, stems removed
a squeeze of lemon juice (optional)
sea salt and freshly ground black pepper

Warm the olive oil and water in a saucepan. Gradually whisk in the grated bottarga over a low heat to form an emulsion – a bit like making taramasalata.

Cook the spaghettini in a large pan of boiling salted water until *al dente*, adding the agretti a minute before the pasta is ready. Drain, reserving a little of the cooking water, and add the pasta and agretti to the bottarga. Toss together and cook over a low heat for 1 minute, adding a spoonful or two of the reserved cooking water to loosen the sauce, if necessary. Adjust the seasoning, being careful with the salt as bottarga can be quite salty. Personally I quite like a squeeze of lemon but a purist would probably disagree.

Fusilli with Cuttlefish, Tomato, Chilli and Parsley

Cuttlefish is available all year round and has a similar flavour to squid. The texture tends to be a little tougher, however, so it's important to buy small cuttlefish and to cut them very, very finely.

The nice thing about this dish is that if you slice the cuttlefish thinly enough it gets stuck between the ridges of the fusilli – plus the classic combination of tomato, chilli and parsley is delicious with the sweet freshness of the cuttlefish.

500g cuttlefish
2 tablespoons olive oil
1 garlic clove, finely sliced
a pinch of dried chilli flakes
100ml dry white wine
400g can of chopped tomatoes
400g fusilli
1 tablespoon chopped flat-leaf parsley
sea salt and freshly ground black pepper

If your fishmonger hasn't already removed the cuttles from inside the cuttlefish, then pull them out (dry them for your budgerigar). Scrape off the tough outer skin of the cuttlefish, exposing the pearly-white flesh. Cut it lengthwise in half and slice it horizontally as finely as you can (the finer you slice it, the more tender it will be). Toss the cuttlefish in a bowl with a tablespoon of the olive oil and some salt and pepper.

Heat a large, heavy-based frying pan. When the pan is really hot, add the cuttlefish and cook for 2 minutes. Add the garlic, chilli and white wine and simmer until the wine has reduced by half. Stir in the tomatoes, reduce the heat and cook slowly for 20 minutes. If there isn't enough liquid in the pan, add a little water.

Cook the fusilli in a large pan of boiling salted water until *al dente*. Drain, add to the sauce in the frying pan and toss well. Add the parsley and the remaining olive oil and leave over a low heat for 2 minutes, so the fusilli can absorb the flavours of the sauce. Toss again and serve.

Spaghetti with Anchovies, Chilli and Garlic

This is the dish to cook when there is virtually nothing in the house except that forgotten tin of anchovies, some garlic and chillies at the bottom of the fridge, and thank goodness for that parsley still growing in the pot on the window ledge.

2 tablespoons olive oil
1 garlic clove, finely sliced
10 salted anchovy fillets in olive oil
1 red chilli, finely sliced
1 tablespoon chopped flat-leaf parsley
½ lemon
400g spaghetti
sea salt and freshly ground black pepper
good olive oil, to serve

Heat the olive oil in a large frying pan, add the sliced garlic and cook gently until soft. Add the anchovies and cook, stirring, until they've broken up, then add the chopped chilli, parsley and a squeeze of lemon. Turn off the heat.

Cook the spaghetti in a large pan of boiling salted water until *al dente*. Drain, reserving a little of the cooking water, and add the pasta to the anchovies, garlic and parsley. Add 2 tablespoonfuls of the pasta water and toss well together over a low heat for a couple of minutes. You will probably not need any extra salt, as the anchovies are salty. Serve with a drizzle of good olive oil and some black pepper.

Tagliatelle with Sea Bass, Zucchini, Basil and Capers

This is a lovely recipe, particularly if you have, as we do in the restaurant, the tail piece of the sea bass. It's not the most popular cut, which is ridiculous, as it has just as much flavour as any other part of the fillet. You don't have to use the tail, of course, but if you're buying filleted fish it should be cheaper than a middle cut.

300g zucchini
3 tablespoons olive oil
1 garlic clove, finely sliced
200g fresh sea bass fillet, skinned and cut into thin strips
8 basil leaves, chopped
1 tablespoon small capers in vinegar, drained
250g fresh tagliatelle (or dried egg tagliatelle)
sea salt and freshly ground black pepper

Cut the zucchini into rounds 1cm thick and then cut them into batons. Heat the olive oil in a large frying pan, add the garlic and cook for 1 minute, until softened. Add the zucchini and cook slowly for 5 minutes, until they are light golden. Add the sea bass strips, basil, capers and some seasoning. Cook for 2–3 minutes, until the sea bass is almost cooked through (if you overcook the fish, it will break up too much). Remove from the heat.

Cook the tagliatelle in a large pan of boiling salted water for about 3 minutes, until *al dente* (or cook according to the packet instructions for dried tagliatelle), then drain, reserving a few tablespoons of the cooking water. Put the sauce back on the heat, add the pasta and toss together. Loosen the sauce with a little of the reserved pasta water if necessary, then cook over a low heat for 2 minutes before serving.

Taglierini with Squid and Ox Heart Tomatoes

The only difficult part of this dish is getting fresh squid – don't use frozen squid. If you go to your fishmonger's the day before, they should be able to order it in fresh. Once the squid is cleaned (and you can ask your fishmonger to do this, as it is a slightly messy job), the only preparation is to slice it as evenly as possible, as this will affect its cooking time and texture. Ox Heart tomatoes are used here because they are very fleshy and give a lightness to the sauce, making this very much a summer pasta.

300g cleaned squid, cut into slices 1cm thick
1 tablespoon olive oil
1 garlic clove, finely sliced
1 red chilli, deseeded and finely chopped
1 tablespoon chopped flat-leaf parsley
3 Ox Heart tomatoes, skinned, deseeded and roughly chopped
250g fresh taglierini
sea salt and freshly ground black pepper

Put the squid in a bowl and toss with the olive oil and some salt and pepper. Place a large, heavy-based frying pan over the highest possible heat and wait for it to start to smoke. Add the sliced squid and cook for 2 minutes, making sure that the squid gets a little colour. Add the garlic, chilli and parsley, then add the tomatoes a handful at a time so the sauce doesn't boil. Turn off the heat when they've all been added.

Cook the taglierini in a large pan of boiling salted water for about 3 minutes, until *al dente*, then drain and add to the squid. Toss well and cook over a low heat for a minute. Season to taste and serve.

Seafood

Seafood

I always think that one of the most enjoyable ways to eat pasta is with seafood. It reminds me of holidays by the sea, where restaurants have that distinctive aroma of mussels, clams, shrimps and prawns being cooked with plenty of garlic and parsley and then tossed together with really superb *al dente* spaghetti.

Shellfish tends to be expensive but certain types, such as mussels and clams, are surprisingly affordable. In the UK, we have some of the best seafood in the world. If you are lucky enough to live on the coast of Scotland, you will be able to buy scallops in the shell and live langoustines for a lot less than you would anywhere else. Scallops and langoustines are probably the sweetest of all seafood, and the most delicious. When I use them in pasta dishes, I like to keep things simple, so you get the full flavour of the main ingredient.

Buying a fresh crab or lobster is a real treat and should be made into a special occasion. They are always best bought live. When you buy them ready cooked, you have no real idea of how old they actually are. This is incredibly important because their flavour deteriorates if you don't eat them fairly soon after cooking. I love lobster but my preference is for crab, because it has more meat and tastes sweeter. If you use the brown meat, which is often considered inferior to white, it will give you so much more flavour. It's a bit like the chicken breast and leg scenario, where the humbler meat is actually the tastier one.

Prawns come in all shapes and sizes and from all corners of the globe. One of my favourite varieties is the brown shrimp, which is becoming much easier to get hold of due to its surge in popularity. Obviously there's a big selection of frozen prawns you can use. Try to buy them with the shell on, as these will have more flavour and cook better than the ones that have had the shell removed before freezing. It's worth looking at the country of origin, as prawns are being overfished due to huge demand. If there is any suggestion that they come from a sustainable source, then try to buy these.

When you prepare shellfish, never soak it in water. All this will do is dilute the flavour and, particularly with something as delicate as a scallop, will make it boil when you cook it. If you are cooking lobsters and crabs, let them cool down at room temperature or in the fridge but don't put them into cold iced water.

Spaghetti with Prawns, Coppa di Parma and Parsley

Coppa di Parma is a ham made from the shoulder of the pig rather than the leg. It is very versatile, as it has a fairly high fat content, and is usually very reasonably priced.

I had a dish similar to this in New York at Mario Batali's Babbo restaurant. The combination of the salty, fatty coppa with the sweet prawns and lots and lots of parsley was inspired.

75g unsalted butter
1 garlic clove, finely sliced
8 slices of coppa di Parma, cut into strips 1cm wide
250g peeled raw prawns, de-veined and cut lengthwise in half
1 fresh green chilli, deseeded and chopped
400g spaghetti
3 tablespoons chopped flat-leaf parsley
sea salt and freshly ground black pepper

Melt the butter in a large frying pan, add the garlic and coppa di Parma and cook gently for 2–3 minutes. Turn up the heat, add the prawns and chilli and cook for 2 minutes, until the prawns are pink. Check the seasoning, but be aware that coppa can be quite salty once it's cooked.

Cook the spaghetti in a large pan of boiling salted water until *al dente*, then drain, reserving a little of the cooking water. Add the pasta to the frying pan, together with 3 tablespoons of the cooking water. Toss together with the parsley and some black pepper and cook over a low heat for 2 minutes.

Spaghetti with Lobster

On a weekend trip to Venice, my wife, Natalie, and I came across a restaurant in St Mark's Square that looked touristy but I knew there was something about it. When the head waiter tried to seat us in the almost-empty, pink-tableclothed dining room I refused, knowing there must be another room somewhere for the locals. The waiter smiled and took us through an alleyway and a kitchen into a stone-clad restaurant packed with people enjoying their lunch. I noticed two businessmen walk in and sit down. They obviously knew the waiter and ordered a dish immediately, then carried on with their solemn business discussions for 20 minutes or so. Eventually two huge plates of pasta appeared. The men's faces lit up – as did mine. They removed their jackets and tucked the biggest napkins you've ever seen into their shirts. As they started eating lobster spaghetti, the business talk coming from the table changed to sounds of sheer enjoyment. It was a wonderful example of how food can transform an atmosphere.

1 x 600g lobster, cooked
3 tablespoons good olive oil
1 garlic clove, finely sliced
250g ripe plum tomatoes, skinned, deseeded and chopped
400g spaghetti
a bunch of flat-leaf parsley, chopped
1 small red chilli, diced
sea salt and freshly ground black pepper

Put the lobster down with the tail flat on a board and, with a sharp, heavy knife, cut lengthwise through the middle of the tail to make 2 half tails. Pull off the head and claws. Crack the claws with a heavy knife and remove the meat, then remove any meat from the head (keep the head and legs, which make fantastic stock or really good soup). Cut the half tails in half again. Keeping the lobster tail in the shell in this way adds flavour to the sauce.

Heat a tablespoon of the olive oil in a pan, add the garlic and cook gently for 1 minute. Stir in the tomatoes and cook rapidly for 5–7 minutes, until the sauce has become thicker and the flavour is concentrated.

Cook the spaghetti in a large pan of boiling salted water until *al dente*. Meanwhile, heat 1 tablespoon of the remaining olive oil in a large frying pan, add the lobster tail quarters, head and claw meat, chopped parsley and red chilli and fry for 1 minute. When the pasta is done, drain and add to the lobster with the tomato sauce. Season, then cook for 2 minutes, tossing constantly, so the pasta can absorb the flavours of the sauce. Add the remaining olive oil and serve immediately.

Vermicelli with Prawns, Tomato and Basil

Vermicelli is a very underused pasta and cooks remarkably quickly; this kind of dish can be made from start to finish in less than 20 minutes. It's delicious in summer, when lovely, ripe plum tomatoes are available.

1 tablespoon olive oil, plus extra to serve
1 garlic clove, finely sliced
1 dried chilli
2 tablespoons chopped basil
300g ripe plum tomatoes, skinned, deseeded and chopped
500g peeled raw prawns, de-veined and cut lengthwise in half
400g vermicelli
sea salt and freshly ground black pepper

Heat the oil in a large, heavy-based frying pan, add the garlic, chilli and half the basil and cook gently until the garlic is soft. Add the tomatoes and cook vigorously for 5–7 minutes, until the sauce has become thicker and the flavour is concentrated. Remove from the heat, add the prawns and let them cook in the residual heat of the sauce. Season to taste.

Cook the pasta in a large pan of boiling salted water until al dente – it will cook very quickly. Drain and add to the sauce, then toss well and cook gently for 2 minutes. Finish with the remaining basil and a good dash of olive oil.

Linguine with Clams, Zucchini and Chilli

This is a variation on a classic spaghetti vongole, but the addition of zucchini and the use of flat linguine make it a real summer treat. I like to use fresh chilli in this recipe, as it has more texture than dried.

1kg clams
3 tablespoons olive oil
1 garlic clove, thinly sliced
a small glass of dry white wine, preferably Soave
2 zucchini, cut into rounds 1cm thick
1 red chilli, deseeded and finely sliced
2 tablespoons chopped flat-leaf parsley
400g linguine
sea salt and freshly ground black pepper
good olive oil, to serve

Wash the clams thoroughly in cold water, discarding any with cracked or open shells, then set aside. Heat half the olive oil in a large saucepan, add the garlic and cook gently for 1–2 minutes, until soft. Add the clams, cover the pan and cook over a fairly high heat for 3–4 minutes. Add the white wine and cook for a further 2 minutes or until all the clams have opened. Scoop out the clams with a slotted spoon and remove them from their shells. Strain the cooking juices through a fine sieve and set aside.

Heat the remaining olive oil in a large frying pan, add the zucchini and fry gently for 5 minutes or until tender. Add the red chilli, parsley and the clams with their strained juices and cook gently for 5 minutes.

Meanwhile, cook the linguine in a large pan of boiling salted water until *al dente*, then drain, reserving a little of the cooking water. Add the pasta to the zucchini and clams, toss well and season to taste. You may need to add a spoonful or two of the reserved pasta water if the sauce looks a little dry. Cook gently for 2 minutes, then serve with a dash of good olive oil and some black pepper.

Pappardelle with Crab, Fennel and Tomatoes

The inspiration for this dish comes from southern Italy, although they would probably use linguine there. The reason I chose pappardelle is that the crab, tomato and fennel sit lightly on it, making a lovely summer dish – but do go for linguine, if you prefer.

2 tablespoons olive oil
2 garlic cloves, finely sliced
400g ripe plum tomatoes, skinned, deseeded and finely chopped
1 fennel bulb, finely sliced
300g fresh pappardelle
1 green chilli, deseeded and finely chopped
300g fresh crabmeat
2 tablespoons chopped flat-leaf parsley
a squeeze of lemon (optional)
sea salt and freshly ground black pepper

Heat a tablespoon of the olive oil in a frying pan, add half the garlic and cook until softened. Add the chopped tomatoes and cook over a high heat for 5–7 minutes, until the sauce has become thicker and the flavour is concentrated. Season and put to one side.

Add the fennel and pappardelle to a large pot of boiling salted water and cook for 3–4 minutes, until the pasta is *al dente*. Meanwhile, heat the remaining olive oil in a large frying pan, add the remaining garlic, plus the green chilli and the crab and cook for 2 minutes. Stir in the tomato sauce and chopped parsley.

Drain the pappardelle and fennel and add them to the sauce. Toss thoroughly and cook for 2 minutes, then serve in shallow bowls, with black pepper and maybe a squeeze of lemon.

Taglierini with Brown Shrimps and Artichokes

This recipe is made with young violet artichokes, which have very little choke inside. When fresh, they are incredibly tender. The combination of brown shrimp, artichoke, butter and chilli is just wonderful.

4 violet artichokes
1 tablespoon olive oil
1 garlic clove, finely sliced
75g unsalted butter
1 dried chilli
100g peeled brown shrimps
2 teaspoons chopped flat-leaf parsley
½ lemon
250g fresh taglierini (or dried egg taglierini)
sea salt and freshly ground black pepper

Peel the artichoke stems, remove the outer leaves, then slice off the top 2cm and scoop out the choke. Cut the artichokes in half and slice them very thinly.

Heat the olive oil in a pan, add the garlic and artichokes and fry gently for about 8 minutes, until softened. Put to one side.

Melt the butter in a large, heavy-based saucepan and add the chilli, brown shrimps and chopped parsley, plus a squeeze of lemon. Cook on a low heat for 2 minutes, then add the artichokes.

Cook the taglierini in a large pan of boiling salted water for about 3 minutes, until *al dente* (or cook according to the packet instructions for dried taglierini). Drain, reserving a few tablespoons of the cooking water, and add to the sauce. Toss together, adding a little of the reserved water to loosen the sauce if necessary. Cook gently for a couple of minutes, adjust the seasoning and serve.

Tagliatelle with Mussels and Saffron

Mussels are very versatile and are always reasonably priced. In my experience, the best ones tend to be those with large, fat shells.

This sauce combines the great flavours of mussel and saffron with the luxurious addition of cream. The mussels can be cooked in advance, making it really quick to finish the dish at the last minute. The juice from the mussels forms the body of the sauce.

1kg mussels, cleaned
2 tablespoons olive oil
1 garlic clove, finely sliced
a pinch of dried chilli flakes
a glass of dry white wine
a pinch of saffron strands
1 tablespoon chopped flat-leaf parsley
75ml double cream
250g fresh tagliatelle (or dried egg tagliatelle)
sea salt and freshly ground black pepper

Give the mussels a good wash and a scrub to remove any barnacles, then pull off the 'beards'. Discard any open mussels.

Put the olive oil, garlic and chilli in a large saucepan with a tight-fitting lid and cook for 1 minute. Add the mussels and put the lid on. Leave over a high heat for 2 minutes, then shake the pan, remove the lid and add the white wine. Cover and cook for another 2–3 minutes, until all the mussels have opened, then take off the heat. Drain off the cooking liquid through a fine sieve and set to one side. Remove the cooked mussels from their shells, discarding any that have refused to open.

Put the cooking liquid, mussels, saffron, parsley and cream in a large saucepan and simmer gently for 3 minutes or until the sauce is thick enough to coat the back of a spoon. Taste and adjust the seasoning.

Cook the tagliatelle in a large pan of boiling salted water for about 3 minutes, until *al dente* (or cook according to the packet instructions for dried tagliatelle). Drain, reserving a few spoonfuls of the cooking water, and add to the sauce. Toss well, adding a little of the reserved water if necessary to loosen the sauce, cook gently for 2 minutes, then serve.

Tagliatelle with Mussels, Rocket and Crème Fraîche

This simple seafood pasta is both tasty and cheap – mussels are reasonably priced and quite easy to obtain. The addition of crème fraîche and rocket makes it a soothing but very flavoursome pasta sauce.

1kg mussels
1 tablespoon olive oil
1 garlic clove, finely sliced
1 red chilli, deseeded and sliced
100ml white wine
100ml crème fraîche
100g wild rocket, roughly chopped
250g fresh tagliatelle (or dried egg tagliatelle)
sea salt and freshly ground black pepper

Give the mussels a good wash and a scrub to remove any barnacles, then pull off the 'beards'. Discard any open mussels.

Heat the olive oil in a large saucepan, add the garlic and chilli and cook gently for 1 minute. Then add the mussels, cover the pan and cook over a high heat for 3 minutes. Shake the pan, remove the lid and add the white wine. Cover and cook for another 3 minutes or until all the mussels have opened. Scoop out the mussels with a slotted spoon and leave to cool. Strain the cooking juices through a fine sieve, discarding the chilli and garlic – they have already given their flavour to the juices. Remove the cooked mussels from their shells, discarding any that have refused to open.

Pour the mussel cooking juices into a saucepan, bring to the boil and simmer until reduced by half. Add the mussels, crème fraîche and finally the chopped rocket, then season to taste.

Cook the tagliatelle in a large pan of boiling salted water for about 3 minutes, until *al dente* (or cook according to the packet instructions for dried tagliatelle). Drain, reserving a little of the cooking water, and add to the sauce. Toss well, adding a little of the water to loosen the sauce if necessary. Cook gently for 2 minutes, then serve.

Taglierini with Scallops, Zucchini, Tomato and Capers

If you can get scallops in the shell, it will make this dish that much more enjoyable. They have a much firmer, sweeter texture than ready-prepared scallops, which are usually quite wet.

When making this dish, it's important to get some colour on the courgettes, as this will add to the flavour.

6 small zucchini
2 tablespoons olive oil
1 garlic clove, finely sliced
8 fresh scallops, sliced
4 fresh plum tomatoes, skinned, deseeded and chopped
1 tablespoon small capers in vinegar, drained
1 tablespoon chopped flat-leaf parsley
250g fresh taglierini (or dried egg taglierini)
sea salt and freshly ground black pepper

Cut the zucchini into rounds 1cm thick and then cut them into batons. Heat the olive oil in a large, heavy-based frying pan, add the garlic, then the zucchini and cook over a medium heat for 10 minutes, until the zucchini are light golden. Add the scallops, raise the heat and fry for 2 minutes, until they have turned a creamy white colour. Stir in the chopped tomatoes, capers and parsley, season to taste and remove from the heat.

Cook the taglierini in a large pan of boiling salted water for about 3 minutes, until *al dente* (or cook according to the packet instructions for dried taglierini). Drain and add to the sauce. Toss together, cook gently for a minute or so, then serve.

Elbow Macaroni with Clams and Artichokes

I discovered this dish in a lovely little restaurant in Rome called Osteria di Romana. The combination of artichoke and clams with the small, curved macaroni was delicious. If you can't get elbow macaroni (also known as chifferi), any macaroni or other small pasta such as farfalle would be fine.

Always buy clams with tightly closed shells – this is a sign that they are alive.

2 Roman artichokes
juice of 1 lemon
3 tablespoons olive oil
1 garlic clove, finely sliced
500g clams
50ml white wine
3 tablespoons chopped flat-leaf parsley
400g elbow macaroni
sea salt and freshly ground black pepper

Prepare the artichokes as described on page 45, slicing them into eighths after soaking them in water acidulated with the lemon juice.

Heat the olive oil in a pan, add the garlic and cook gently for 1 minute. Add the artichokes and half a glass of water, cover and cook over a low heat for 10 minutes, until the artichokes are tender. Season with salt and pepper.

Wash the clams thoroughly in cold water, discarding any with cracked or open shells, then set aside. Place a large pan over a high heat, add the clams, white wine and parsley, then cover and cook for 3–4 minutes, until all the clams have opened. Leave to cool, then strain through a fine sieve, reserving the cooking juices. Remove the clams from their shells, leaving a few in their shells to look pretty. Add all the clams to the artichokes with their cooking juices.

Cook the pasta in a large pan of boiling salted water until *al dente,* then drain, reserving a little of the cooking water. Add the pasta to the artichokes, together with a spoonful or two of the pasta water to loosen the sauce if necessary. Toss together and cook over a low heat for 2 minutes. Adjust the seasoning and serve.

Spaghetti with Brown Shrimps, Peas and Pancetta

Brown shrimps are available ready peeled and are easy to get from most fishmongers. The addition of pancetta makes this dish really tasty, while the peas add colour and texture.

1 tablespoon olive oil
75g pancetta, cut into matchsticks
1 garlic clove, finely sliced
200g fresh or frozen peas
100g brown shrimps
1 small dried chilli, deseeded and crumbled
1 tablespoon chopped flat-leaf parsley
75ml double cream
400g spaghetti
sea salt and freshly ground black pepper

Heat the olive oil in a large frying pan, add the pancetta and cook until crisp. Drain off excess fat, then add the garlic and cook for 1 minute. Add the peas – if frozen, put them straight in; if fresh, blanch them in boiling salted water for 2 minutes first. Stir in the shrimps, dried chilli, parsley and cream, cook gently for 3–4 minutes, then season well.

Cook the spaghetti in a large pan of boiling salted water until *al dente*, then drain, reserving a little of the cooking water. Add the pasta to the shrimps and peas, toss well and add a few spoonfuls of the pasta water to make the sauce juicy.

Linguine with Crab, Peas and Crème Fraîche

There are few things more rewarding than cooking a live crab and picking the meat yourself. The flavour is far superior to anything you can buy. Generally most pre-picked crabmeat has been pasteurised, meaning that it loses all of its sweet crab flavour, which for me is the whole point. I like to use male brown crabs from Cornwall or Devon. If you really aren't keen on cooking it yourself, a good fishmonger will sell you a freshly cooked one.

1 tablespoon olive oil
1 garlic clove, finely sliced
1 green chilli, chopped
50g fresh brown crabmeat
200g fresh white crabmeat
½ lemon
1 tablespoon chopped flat-leaf parsley
150ml crème fraîche
400g linguine
200g podded small fresh peas
sea salt and freshly ground black pepper

Heat the olive oil in a large frying pan, add the garlic and cook gently until soft. Add the green chilli and brown crabmeat and cook for 1 minute, then add the white crabmeat. Stir well and season with a squeeze of lemon and some salt and pepper. Add the chopped parsley and cook for 2 minutes, then stir in the crème fraîche and turn off the heat.

Add the linguine to a large pan of boiling salted water and cook until *al dente*, adding the peas after 4 minutes. Drain, add to the crab sauce, toss well and cook gently for a couple of minutes. Season with black pepper and serve.

Taglierini with Seafood and Tomato

This is an all-time holiday favourite. The ingredients can be varied depending on what's available but I would always suggest you use mussels, as they have loads of flavour.

16 mussels
20 small clams
4 tablespoons olive oil
2 garlic cloves, finely sliced
400g can of chopped tomatoes
a glass of white wine
250g cleaned squid, finely sliced
100g peeled brown shrimps
1 tablespoon chopped flat-leaf parsley
a pinch of dried chilli flakes
250g fresh taglierini (or dried egg taglierini)
sea salt and freshly ground black pepper

Give the mussels a good wash and a scrub to remove any barnacles, then pull off the 'beards'. Discard any open mussels. Wash the clams thoroughly in cold water, discarding any with cracked or open shells.

Heat a tablespoon of the olive oil in a heavy-based saucepan, add a third of the garlic and cook for 1 minute. Add the chopped tomatoes, bring to the boil and simmer for 10 minutes, until reduced. Season to taste, remove from the heat and set aside.

Divide 2 tablespoons of the remaining oil and all the remaining garlic between 2 pans with tight-fitting lids and cook gently for a minute or so, until the garlic has softened. Add the mussels to one pan and the clams to the other, then cover and cook for 2 minutes over a fairly high heat. Add half the white wine to each pan, cover again and leave for 3–4 minutes, until all the mussels and clams have opened. Remove the shellfish from the pans, take them out of their shells and set aside. Tip all the cooking juices into one pan, bring to the boil and simmer until reduced by half.

Heat the remaining tablespoon of olive oil in a large frying pan, add the sliced squid and cook over a high heat for 2 minutes. The squid should have a little colour on it. Add the mussels and clams, their reduced cooking juices, the shrimps, parsley, chilli and some seasoning. Then add the tomato sauce, turn the heat down and stir together.

Cook the taglierini in a large pan of boiling salted water for about 3 minutes, until *al dente* (or cook according to the packet instructions for dried taglierini). Drain and add to the sauce, toss well and cook gently for 2 minutes. Finish with black pepper.

Prepare the artichokes as described on page 45, slicing them into eighths after soaking them in water acidulated with the lemon juice.

Tagliatelle with Clams, White Asparagus and Parsley

This is an unusual combination. I remember having a similar dish with Rose Gray from The River Café when eating lunch at a restaurant in Verona called L'Oste Scuro. We were both blown away by the inclusion of cinnamon with the clams and white asparagus.

200g white asparagus, trimmed
500g clams
1 tablespoon olive oil
1 garlic clove, finely sliced
100ml dry white wine, preferably Soave
75g unsalted butter, diced
1 tablespoon chopped flat-leaf parsley
a pinch of ground cinnamon
250g fresh tagliatelle (or dried egg tagliatelle)
sea salt and freshly ground black pepper

Cook the asparagus in a large pan of boiling salted water until tender, then drain and leave to cool. Slice at a slight angle, 1cm thick, and set aside.

Wash the clams thoroughly in cold water, discarding any with cracked or open shells, then set aside.

Heat a heavy-based saucepan, add the oil and garlic and cook gently for 1 minute, until the garlic is soft but not coloured. Add the clams, cover the pan and cook over a high heat for 2 minutes. Then add the white wine, cover again and cook for a minute or two longer, until all the clams have opened. Drain through a fine sieve, reserving the liquid. Take all the clams out of their shells and set aside.

Pour the reserved cooking liquid into a large frying pan and bring to the boil. Add the asparagus and clams, turn off the heat and slowly stir in the butter so you get an emulsified sauce. Add the parsley and cinnamon and season to taste.

Cook the tagliatelle in a large pan of boiling salted water for about 3 minutes, until *al dente* (or cook according to the packet instructions for dried tagliatelle). Drain and add to the sauce. Toss well, cook together gently for a couple of minutes, then serve with black pepper.

Taglierini with Shrimps and Zucchini

Brown shrimps have a salty-sweet taste that is delicious with the gentle flavour of zucchini. This is one of those very quick sauces that can be made in the time the pasta takes to cook.

250g fresh taglierini
3 small zucchini, grated
100g unsalted butter
1 garlic clove, finely sliced
1 dried chilli, deseeded and crushed
150g peeled brown shrimps
freshly ground black pepper

Put the taglierini and grated zucchini in a large pan of boiling salted water and cook for about 3 minutes, until the pasta is *al dente*. Meanwhile, melt the butter in a frying pan, add the garlic and chilli and fry for a couple of minutes, then stir in the brown shrimps. Season to taste.

When the pasta and zucchini are cooked, drain and add to the butter and shrimps. Toss really well and serve with some black pepper.

Spaghetti with Lobster, Fennel, Tomatoes and Zucchini

Lobster is considered the king of shellfish but it can be disappointing when you buy it pre-cooked. In my experience, the best lobsters are the native Scottish ones or the Dorset Blue lobster, which is an almost electric blue before it is cooked. When I buy a lobster, I always ask for some seaweed, which is put on top of the lobster in its polystyrene box. The seaweed tends to keep the lobster calm while it is stored in the fridge.

1 x 600g lobster, cooked
2 small zucchini, cut into slices 5mm thick
1 fennel bulb, cut into slices 5mm thick
2 tablespoons olive oil
1 garlic clove, finely sliced
400g can of chopped tomatoes
1 tablespoon chopped flat-leaf parsley
400g spaghetti
sea salt and freshly ground black pepper

Put the lobster down with the tail flat on a board and, with a sharp, heavy knife, cut lengthwise through the middle of the tail to make 2 half tails. Pull off the head and claws. Crack the claws with a heavy knife and remove the meat, then remove any meat from the head (the head and claws can be kept to make soup or stock). Cut each half tail into 3 pieces – leaving the tail in the shell in this way will add flavour to the sauce.

Cook the zucchini and fennel in a pan of boiling salted water until tender but not mushy, then drain and set aside.

Heat the olive oil in a saucepan, add the garlic and cook gently until soft. Add the tomatoes and cook slowly for 10 minutes. Add the lobster, zucchini, fennel and chopped parsley, season well and add a dash of good olive oil.

Cook the spaghetti in a large pan of boiling salted water until *al dente*, then drain. Add to the lobster sauce, toss well and cook gently for a couple of minutes. Serve with black pepper.

Gnocchi with Langoustines, Tomato and Cream

Langoustines are probably my favourite shellfish of all, but can be hard to get hold of. Ideally, this recipe would be made with fresh langoustines – or better still, live ones that you boil yourself, but you're more likely to find them cooked and frozen. If you're in Scotland it's a great dish to make, because langoustines are easily available there and don't cost the earth – unlike in London, sadly.

If you can't get hold of langoustines, a good alternative is live crayfish, a freshwater crustacean. Any decent fishmonger should be able to order some for you.

2 tablespoons olive oil
1 garlic clove, finely sliced
a pinch of dried chilli flakes
300g peeled cooked langoustines
10 basil leaves, chopped
50ml dry white wine
250g ripe plum tomatoes, skinned, deseeded and chopped
50ml double cream
500g potato gnocchi
sea salt and freshly ground black pepper

Heat the olive oil in a large frying pan, add the garlic, dried chilli, langoustines and basil and cook for 2 minutes over a high heat, until there's a little colour on the langoustines. Add the white wine and simmer until reduced by half. Add the tomatoes and cook for 5 minutes. Add the cream and cook for a minute longer.

Add the gnocchi to a large pan of boiling salted water and cook for 2–3 minutes, until they rise to the top of the pan. Remove with a slotted spoon, drain and add to the sauce, together with a spoonful or two of the gnocchi cooking liquid to loosen the sauce if necessary. Toss together gently, season and serve.

Tagliatelle with Mussels, Radicchio and Pangrattato

This is an interesting pasta sauce as the bitterness of radicchio gives it much more depth than you might expect. The combination of sweet mussels and cream with a scattering of crispy pangrattato makes a very satisfying mouthful.

100ml sunflower oil
2 slices of stale ciabatta, whizzed to crumbs in a food processor
1kg mussels
2 tablespoons olive oil
2 garlic cloves, finely sliced
150ml white wine, preferably Soave
1 head of radicchio, shredded
juice of 1 lemon
100ml double cream
1 tablespoon chopped flat-leaf parsley
250g fresh tagliatelle (or dried egg tagliatelle)
sea salt and freshly ground black pepper

To make the pangrattato, heat the sunflower oil to about 170°C in a small saucepan, add the breadcrumbs and fry until golden brown. Remove with a slotted spoon, drain on kitchen paper and season with salt and pepper.

Give the mussels a good wash and a scrub to remove any barnacles, then pull off the 'beards'. Discard any open mussels.

Heat half the olive oil in a large, heavy-based pan, add half the garlic and cook gently until soft. Add the mussels and white wine, cover the pan and cook over a high heat until all the mussels have opened. Strain the juices through a fine sieve and keep to one side. Remove the mussels from their shells.

Heat the remaining olive oil in a large frying pan, add the remaining garlic and cook gently until softened. Add the radicchio and cook for 10 minutes or until it has wilted, like cooked cabbage. Add the mussel cooking juices and bring to the boil. Add the lemon juice, double cream, parsley and cooked mussels and heat through gently. Season to taste.

Cook the tagliatelle in a large pan of boiling salted water for about 3 minutes, until *al dente* (or cook according to the packet instructions for dried tagliatelle). Drain and add to the sauce, toss well and cook for a minute so the pasta absorbs some of the juices. Serve with the pangrattato on top.

Tagliatelle with Brown Shrimps, Asparagus and Pancetta

When mixed with butter, brown shrimps have an incredible flavour and are strong enough to withstand robust ingredients such as pancetta and chilli, yet mild enough not to overwhelm the more gentle taste of the asparagus.

300g asparagus, trimmed
1 tablespoon olive oil
1 garlic clove, finely sliced
100g pancetta, cut into matchsticks
a pinch of dried chilli flakes
150g brown shrimps
1 tablespoon chopped flat-leaf parsley
75g unsalted butter
250g fresh tagliatelle (or dried egg tagliatelle)
sea salt and freshly ground black pepper

Cook the asparagus in a large pan of boiling salted water until tender, then drain and leave to cool. Cut it at an angle into slices 1cm thick and set aside.

Heat the olive oil in a large frying pan, add the garlic and cook gently until softened. Add the pancetta and cook until golden brown. Drain off any excess fat, then add the sliced asparagus, dried chilli, brown shrimps and chopped parsley. Add the butter and stir together but don't cook any longer.

Cook the tagliatelle in a large pan of boiling salted water for about 3 minutes, until *al dente* (or cook according to the packet instructions for dried tagliatelle). Drain, keeping back a little of the pasta water, and toss with the sauce, adding a spoonful or two of the pasta water to loosen it. Cook over a low heat for a minute or so, then serve with black pepper.

Ravioli with Lobster, Fennel and Tomato

This is definitely a special-occasion pasta. Try to make it in summertime, when lobsters are widely available and a lot cheaper. The combination of fennel and tomato is perfect with the sweet taste of the lobster.

1 x 600g lobster, cooked
1 fennel bulb, sliced
1 tablespoon olive oil
1 garlic clove, finely sliced
250g plum tomatoes, skinned, deseeded and finely chopped
4 tablespoons breadcrumbs
½ quantity of Pasta Dough (see page 13)
8 basil leaves, torn
sea salt and freshly ground black pepper
good olive oil, to serve

Remove the head from the lobster and scoop out any meat. Remove the claws, crack them with a heavy knife and pick out all the meat, then take out the meat from the tail. Finely chop all the lobster meat and set aside.

Cook the fennel in boiling salted water until tender, then drain and chop finely. Set aside.
Heat the olive oil in a large frying pan, add the garlic and cook gently until soft. Add the chopped tomatoes and cook for about 10 minutes over a high heat, until they reach a sauce consistency. Season to taste.

Put the chopped lobster, fennel, breadcrumbs and half the tomato sauce in a bowl, mix well and season to taste. If the mixture seems a little wet, add a few more breadcrumbs.

Roll out the pasta dough and make the ravioli as described on page 16. Add the ravioli to a large pan of boiling salted water and simmer for 3–5 minutes, until *al dente*. Meanwhile, reheat the remaining tomato sauce. Drain the ravioli and toss with the tomato sauce and the torn basil. Finish with a dash of good olive oil and plenty of black pepper.

Meat

Meat

Meat sauces tend to be hearty and robust, designed for cold, wintry nights, but not all the recipes in this chapter are strictly for winter. For instance, Spaghetti with Polpettine, Prosciutto and Peas (see page 176) is a great spring dish, as is the Ravioli with Pancetta, Swiss Chard, Ricotta and Chilli (see page 164). Traditionally meat sauces are made using tough cuts of meat or trimmings from prime cuts, but I have included a recipe that uses beef fillet (see page 174), which doesn't require much cooking at all, as it's already very tender. Most meat sauces, however, rely on slow, even cooking, which tenderises and flavours the meat. Generally the tougher cuts have more flavour when slow cooked than the prime cuts. Beef and veal are very good with the addition of artichoke or dried porcini mushrooms, as both of these ingredients complement the richness of the meat – particularly in Rigatoni with Veal and Artichokes (see page 168), which includes milk for a deliciously comforting sauce. Agnolotti with Beef and Porcini (see page 165) is a must-try dish if you've never made your own stuffed pasta, as it's really easy.

Pork is an indispensable part of pasta cookery but in the form of cured pork products, such as sausages, pancetta and prosciutto, rather than fresh pork. The main reason for this is that they accentuate the seasoning of the sauce and add depth of flavour. Italy is famous for its cured pork but one of the most enjoyable cured meats is bresaola, made with beef. I have taken advantage of its deep flavour in Penne with Bresaola, Radicchio and Cream (see page 162).

One of my favourite ways of making pasta sauces is using good-quality Italian sausages. The better the quality, the more flavour they have. My particular favourites are the ones with fennel seeds in. When you cook the sausages without their skins, a lot of fat comes out, leaving a beautifully seasoned mince. The addition of pancetta intensifies the flavour, inviting the idea of adding something fresh and green like Swiss chard or cavolo nero, which makes it a much more balanced sauce.

One of life's true luxuries is a really good spaghetti carbonara, which can be delicious or disastrous, depending how confident you are with your eggs and cream. The real key to a good carbonara, however, is the quality of the pancetta and how much you've cooked it. The crisper the better.

Penne with Bresaola, Radicchio and Cream

Classically, this would probably be made with pancetta, but the addition of bresaola, which is cured beef, gives it an interesting flavour – something that reminds me of Verona, where you often find beef and radicchio together.

2 tablespoons olive oil
1 garlic clove, finely sliced
1 small red onion, finely sliced
1 tablespoon chopped rosemary
1 head of radicchio
12 slices of bresaola, cut into strips
100ml double cream
½ lemon
400g penne rigate
sea salt and freshly ground black pepper
freshly grated Parmesan cheese, to serve

Heat the olive oil in a large, heavy-based saucepan, add the garlic and onion and cook gently until soft. Stir in the chopped rosemary.

Cut the radicchio lengthwise in half and shred it into fine strips (like cabbage). Add to the onion and garlic and cook, uncovered, over a low heat for about 15 minutes, until it has completely wilted. Add half the bresaola (adding some of it at this stage will give the sauce a meaty seasoning) and cook for 5 minutes. Stir in the cream and a squeeze of lemon and cook for 5 minutes longer. Season to taste.

Cook the penne in a large pan of boiling salted water until *al dente*. Drain, reserving a few spoonfuls of the cooking water, and add to the sauce. Toss together well, adding a little of the reserved water to loosen the sauce, if necessary, then cook over a low heat for 2 minutes. Sprinkle over the remaining strips of bresaola and serve with freshly grated Parmesan and some black pepper.

Ravioli with Pancetta, Swiss Chard, Ricotta and Chilli

This is quite a light ravioli, and the Swiss chard and ricotta cheese make it subtle rather than overpowering. The chilli adds that little kick you always need with Swiss chard.

750g Swiss chard
1 tablespoon olive oil
1 garlic clove, finely sliced
1 small red onion, finely chopped
1 dried red chilli, deseeded and crumbled
100g pancetta, cut into matchsticks
a pinch of grated nutmeg
250g ricotta cheese
½ quantity of Pasta Dough (see page 13)
75g unsalted butter
6 sage leaves
sea salt and freshly ground black pepper
freshly grated Parmesan cheese, to serve

Separate the green leaves of the Swiss chard from the stems. Cut the stems into slices 1cm thick and cook in boiling salted water until soft. Remove with a slotted spoon and leave to cool in a colander. Add the chard leaves to the boiling water and cook briefly until tender. Drain, leave to cool, then finely chop the leaves and stalks.

Heat the olive oil in a frying pan, add the garlic, onion and red chilli and cook until soft. Add the pancetta and cook until golden. Stir in the cooked chard, season and add a little grated nutmeg. Remove from the pan and leave to cool. Mix in the ricotta and check the seasoning.

Roll out the pasta dough and make the ravioli as described on page 16. Add the ravioli to a large pan of boiling salted water and simmer for 3–5 minutes, until *al dente*. Meanwhile, melt the butter in a frying pan, add the sage leaves and cook gently together so they infuse, but don't let the butter brown. Drain the pasta and toss with the sage butter. Serve with grated Parmesan and black pepper.

Agnolotti with Beef and Porcini

These little pasta parcels are surprisingly easy to make. Beef and porcini are natural partners, and using a cheaper cut such as chuck makes this an affordable dish.

400g beef chuck, cut into 3cm dice
2 tablespoons olive oil
1 tablespoon finely chopped celery
1 tablespoon finely chopped onion
1 teaspoon chopped thyme
75g dried porcini mushrooms, soaked in hot water for 10 minutes
100ml red wine
½ quantity of Pasta Dough (see page 13)
75g unsalted butter
sea salt and freshly ground black pepper
freshly grated Parmesan cheese, to serve

Season the beef chuck with salt and pepper. Heat the olive oil in a casserole, add the beef and cook until it has a good light brown colour. Remove from the pan and set aside. Add the celery, onion and thyme to the casserole and cook gently for 3–4 minutes, until softened. Strain the porcini through a fine sieve, reserving the soaking water. Add the porcini and their water to the pan, then return the beef to the pan, add the red wine and bring to a simmer. Cover with a tight-fitting lid and transfer to an oven preheated to 160°C/Gas Mark 3. Cook for about 1 hour and 20 minutes, until the beef breaks up easily – check it after 45 minutes to see if you have enough liquid in the pan, and add a little water if necessary.

When the beef is cooked, leave it to cool, then use a slotted spoon to take it out of the pan with the porcini. Place on a chopping board and cut up finely, then return to the casserole. Season to taste. If you feel there is too much cooking liquid, don't use it all as it will make the pasta filling too wet.

Roll out the pasta dough and make the agnolotti as described on page 17. Cook in a large pan of boiling salted water for 3–4 minutes, until *al dente*. Meanwhile, soften the butter in a large frying pan without letting it melt completely. Drain the pasta and toss with the butter. If you have any of the beef cooking juices left, heat them up and toss them with the agnolotti and butter. Serve with Parmesan cheese.

Penne with Sausage, Pancetta and Swiss Chard

This is a really delicious way of using spicy Italian sausages. The addition of Swiss chard gives it a lovely texture, particularly if you include the stalks, and makes it not quite as rich as a classic sausage pasta sauce.

about 800g Swiss chard
2 tablespoons olive oil
1 small onion, finely chopped
1 garlic clove, finely sliced
75g sliced pancetta, cut into matchsticks
150g Tuscan sausages, skinned and finely chopped
50ml double cream
a pinch of dried chilli flakes
400g penne rigate
sea salt and freshly ground black pepper
freshly grated Parmesan cheese, to serve

Trim the ends of the Swiss chard and then cut the green leaves off the white stems. Cut the stems into fine matchsticks and blanch in boiling salted water until soft. Drain and set aside. Blanch the green leaves for 4–5 minutes, then drain and chop roughly.

Heat the olive oil in a large, heavy-based saucepan, add the onion and garlic and cook gently for 5 minutes or until soft. Add the pancetta and sausage meat and cook slowly for 20 minutes. Drain off excess fat. Add the cream to the sauce and bring to the boil. Stir in the dried chilli and the blanched Swiss chard stalks and their leaves, then cook gently for 4 minutes. Season to taste.

Cook the penne in a large pan of boiling salted water until *al dente*, then drain, reserving a few spoonfuls of the cooking water. Add the pasta to the sauce, toss well and add a little of the reserved water if necessary to loosen the sauce. Cook gently for 2 minutes, then serve with black pepper, grated Parmesan and most definitely a glass of good Chianti.

Rigatoni with Veal and Artichokes

The inspiration for this came from the filling for our cappelletti (see page 179). When we made it for the first time, it came out of the oven looking so amazing that I thought it should be cooked with pasta rather than stuffed inside it. Here, I've added artichokes and some milk, which curdles slightly when cooked with the veal, adding a lovely, nutty flavour. The sauce can be made a day in advance and, if you don't feel like pasta, you could serve it with polenta instead.

You can now buy very good, humanely reared British veal that has a distinctive flavour and doesn't cost the earth. I find Waitrose has a good selection of fresh British meat that is surprisingly reasonably priced.

3 tablespoons olive oil
300g veal flank or shoulder, finely chopped
1 small red onion, chopped
1 garlic clove, finely sliced
2 celery sticks, chopped
1 teaspoon chopped rosemary
6 small artichokes
juice of 1 lemon
½ glass of dry white wine
200ml milk
400g rigatoni
75g Parmesan cheese, freshly grated
sea salt and freshly ground black pepper

Heat the oil in a large, heavy-based saucepan, add the chopped veal and cook until lightly browned all over. Remove from the pan and set aside. Add the onion, garlic, celery and rosemary to the pan and cook gently for 5 minutes.

Prepare the artichokes as described on page 45, cutting them into quarters after soaking them in water acidulated with the lemon juice. Add them to the pan, cook for 5 minutes, then return the veal to the pan with the white wine and milk. Bring to a simmer, cover and cook gently for about 1½ hours, until the meat can be broken very easily with a fork. The sauce will probably have curdled slightly but this is a good sign. Season to taste and set aside.

Cook the rigatoni in a large pan of boiling salted water until *al dente*, then drain. Add to the sauce, toss together and cook over a low heat for a couple of minutes. Mix in the grated Parmesan and serve.

Spaghetti with Pancetta, Garlic and Pecorino

The best place to buy pancetta is in an Italian delicatessen, as it will be cut from a whole piece and sliced properly on a meat slicer. If you don't have a deli nearby, you can always use dry-cured streaky bacon, but it will not have the same consistency as pancetta. Italians take pig farming very seriously and the pancetta tradition goes back centuries, making it subject to strict controls.

1 tablespoon olive oil
1 garlic clove, finely sliced
a pinch of dried chilli flakes
150g pancetta, cut into matchsticks
400g spaghetti
150g pecorino toscano cheese, grated
sea salt and freshly ground black pepper

Heat the olive oil in a large frying pan, add the garlic and chilli and cook gently until the garlic is soft. Add the pancetta and cook until golden brown. Drain off excess fat.

Cook the spaghetti in a large pan of boiling salted water until *al dente*, then drain, reserving a little of the cooking water. Add the spaghetti to the frying pan together with 2–3 tablespoons of the reserved cooking water and the grated pecorino. Season to taste. Toss together over a low heat for a couple of minutes so the cheese melts and coats the pasta. Serve with black pepper and a glass of decent Chianti.

Penne with Italian Sausage, Porcini Mushrooms and Tomato

Made with tasty, fatty, meaty Italian sausages, this is a pretty rich sauce. Italian sausages are generally a combination of raw and cured meat. There are so many recipes like this one, where you take off the skin and use the sausage meat as mince, that it's almost as if they were never intended to be sausages.

Fennel seed and chilli are a classic seasoning for Italian sausage, and a personal favourite of mine.

4 tablespoons olive oil
1 small red onion, finely chopped
1 garlic clove, finely sliced
200g Italian sausages, skinned and finely chopped
a pinch of dried red chilli flakes
a pinch of crushed fennel seeds
25g dried porcini mushrooms, soaked in hot water for 10 minutes, then drained
400g can of chopped tomatoes
5 tablespoons double cream
400g penne rigate
sea salt and freshly ground black pepper
grated Parmesan or mature pecorino cheese, to serve

Heat the olive oil in a large saucepan, add the onion and garlic and cook gently until soft. Add the sausage meat and fry over a medium heat for about 10 minutes, until lightly coloured. There may be quite a lot of fat, so drain off the excess. Add the dried chilli, fennel seeds, drained porcini mushrooms and canned tomatoes and simmer for 20–30 minutes, until the sauce has a thick, rich consistency. Stir in the double cream, cook for 3 minutes, then season to taste.

Cook the penne in a large pan of boiling salted water until *al dente*. Drain, add to the sauce and toss together. Cook gently for 2 minutes, then serve with grated Parmesan or pecorino.

Spaghetti Carbonara

There aren't many ingredients here, so it's particularly important that they are all top quality. If you use decent pancetta and good eggs, the end result will be that much more delicious. Don't forget – plenty of black pepper.

100g sliced pancetta, cut into matchsticks
5 organic egg yolks
150ml double cream
400g spaghetti
150g Parmesan cheese, freshly grated, plus extra to serve
freshly ground black pepper

Cook the pancetta in a frying pan until golden brown and very crisp. Drain on kitchen paper and leave to one side.

In a medium bowl, mix together the egg yolks and cream. Put this bowl over a pan of simmering water, making sure the water doesn't touch the base of the bowl, and stir constantly so the eggs don't scramble. Meanwhile, cook the spaghetti in a large pan of boiling salted water until *al dente*. Drain and add to the egg yolks and cream. Toss well, then add the Parmesan and pancetta. If the egg doesn't seem cooked enough from the heat of the spaghetti, place the bowl back over the simmering water and cook for a further 2 minutes, until the mixture coats the spaghetti. Serve with more Parmesan and plenty of black pepper.

Pappardelle with Beef Fillet

This is surprisingly quick for a meat sauce as it uses beef fillet, which doesn't require much cooking. You could substitute other cuts, such as sirloin or rump, but they will take a little longer to cook. The addition of tomato makes this a very satisfying, simple pasta.

2 tablespoons olive oil
1 small red onion, finely chopped
2 celery sticks, finely chopped
1 garlic clove, finely sliced
1 teaspoon chopped rosemary
150g beef fillet, cut into fine strips
150ml red wine, preferably Chianti
400g can of chopped tomatoes
250g fresh pappardelle (or dried egg pappardelle)
50g unsalted butter
sea salt and freshly ground black pepper

Heat the olive oil in a frying pan, add the onion, celery, garlic and rosemary and cook gently until softened. Turn up the heat, add the strips of beef fillet and cook briefly until browned. Add the red wine and chopped tomatoes, bring to a simmer, then cook gently for 20–25 minutes, until the sauce is thick and rich. Season to taste.

Cook the pappardelle in a large pan of boiling salted water for 3–4 minutes, until *al dente* (or cook according to the packet instructions for dried pappardelle). Drain and add to the sauce. Toss well and fold in the butter.

Spaghetti with Polpettine, Prosciutto and Peas

Polpettine are tiny veal meatballs. Their flavour is not as heavy as that of beef meatballs, and adding peas makes this quite a light, spring-like dish.

400g minced veal
100g prosciutto, finely chopped
1 teaspoon chopped mint
1 teacup of dried breadcrumbs
1 organic egg yolk
75g Parmesan cheese, freshly grated, plus extra to serve
2 tablespoons olive oil
75ml double cream
400g spaghetti
200g shelled new-season peas
sea salt and freshly ground black pepper

Place the veal, prosciutto, mint, breadcrumbs, egg yolk and Parmesan cheese in a large bowl and mix together thoroughly with your hands. Add seasoning, then roll the mixture into little balls about 4cm across.

Heat the olive oil in a large frying pan and add the meatballs one by one, making sure they are not too close to each other. Cook carefully, turning over each ball individually so they cook evenly, for about 10 minutes, until cooked through. Drain any excess fat from the pan, then add the double cream and cook gently for 5 minutes.

Cook the spaghetti in a large pan of boiling salted water, adding the peas after 4 minutes. When the pasta is *al dente*, drain and toss with the meatballs. Cook over a low heat for a couple of minutes, then serve with black pepper and Parmesan.

Penne Rigate with Italian Sausages, Cavolo Nero and Cream

This sauce has an amazing bright green colour, thanks to the cavolo nero, which translates as black cabbage. It isn't actually black, just very dark green. It is quite common now in the UK – thanks to Rose and Ruthie at The River Café, who ensured that enough seeds were brought back from various trips to Italy for British farmers they knew to start growing it. The fennel seeds and chilli are very important in this dish, as they season the sauce.

1 tablespoon olive oil
1 garlic clove, finely sliced
300g Italian sausages
a pinch of crushed fennel seeds
a pinch of dried chilli flakes
2 bunches of cavolo nero (about 800g), stems removed
150ml double cream
400g penne rigate
100g Parmesan cheese, freshly grated
sea salt and freshly ground black pepper

Heat the olive oil in a large frying pan, add the garlic and cook until softened. Meanwhile, remove the skins from the sausages and chop the meat finely. Add the crushed fennel seeds and chilli to the pan, then add the sausage meat and cook slowly for about 20 minutes, until light golden. Remove any excess fat and turn off the heat.

Cook the cavolo nero in boiling salted water until tender. Drain, reserving a little of the cooking liquid, and chop roughly. Add the cavolo nero to the sausages with a couple of spoonfuls of its cooking water and turn the heat back on. Add the cream and cook slowly for 10 minutes. Season to taste.

Cook the penne in a large pan of boiling salted water until *al dente*, then drain, reserving a few spoonfuls of the cooking water. Add the pasta to the sausage sauce, together with a little of the reserved cooking water if necessary to loosen the sauce. Stir in the Parmesan, toss well and serve.

Veal Cappelletti

Cappelletti are a slightly larger version of tortellini. This dish has been on the menu in the restaurant from day one, as we always serve veal chops and we use the flank of the loin to make this pasta. The more you prove the pasta dough by passing it through the machine, the finer you can roll it, making a more delicate dish.

300g veal flank, trimmed of excess fat and cut into 3 equal pieces
1 tablespoon olive oil
100g pancetta, chopped
1 celery stick, finely chopped
2 carrots, finely chopped
1 onion, finely chopped
a glass of white wine
100g Parmesan cheese, freshly grated, plus extra to serve
½ quantity of Pasta Dough (see page 13)
75g unsalted butter
sea salt and freshly ground black pepper

Season the veal with salt and pepper. Heat the oil in a casserole, add the seasoned veal and cook until light golden. Remove from the pan, add the pancetta, celery, carrots and onion and cook for 10 minutes or until the pancetta is golden. Return the veal to the pan, add the white wine, cover with foil or a tight-fitting lid and transfer to an oven preheated to 160°C/Gas Mark 3. Cook for 1½ hours or until the veal is very tender. Remove the veal and vegetables from the pan and chop very finely by hand. Season to taste, then add the Parmesan and enough of the cooking juices to give a moist, but not wet mixture. (*Continues overleaf.*)

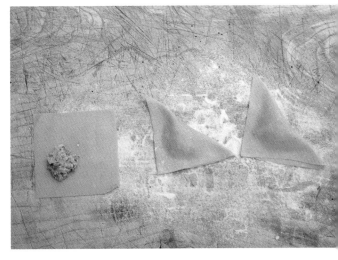

Roll out the pasta dough as thinly as your pasta machine will let you. Cut out 8cm squares and place a teaspoonful of the mixture on each one. Brush the pasta edges with water, then fold in half so you have a triangle. Bring the 2 opposite points of the triangle together and squeeze tight. Repeat this process until you have used up all the filling. The cappelletti can be cooked straight away or kept in the fridge on a floured tray for up to 2 days.

Add the cappelletti to a large pan of boiling salted water and cook for 3–5 minutes, until *al dente*. Meanwhile, soften the butter in a large frying pan, but don't let it melt completely. Drain the pasta and toss with the butter. Serve with Parmesan and black pepper.

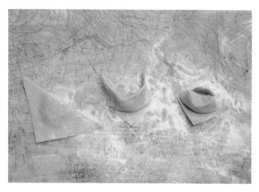 

Poultry
and
Game

Poultry and Game

In the UK we have some of the best game in the world, particularly feathered game such as partridge, pheasant and pigeon. When cooked slowly with herbs and pancetta, these birds create the most amazing pasta sauce. The cooking juices intensify in flavour and, once the bird is cooked, all the meat comes off the bone easily and can then be flaked and mixed with the juices, making a deliciously pungent, gamey sauce. Something quite bland, like a rabbit, can be transformed by braising it with a few basic vegetables such as carrot, celery and onion, plus pancetta, tomatoes and white wine, then finished with a dash of double cream, making this mild meat into a dish packed full of flavour.

Pheasant and woodpigeon are probably the best value of all game. They make a very good stuffing for ravioli or agnolotti (see page 186). The great thing about game-stuffed pastas is that the meat is quite strong, particularly when mixed with grated Parmesan, so you need use only a little.

When I go to Rome, I love to eat Tagliatelle alla Romana (see page 192), which is a very simple preparation of onion, chicken livers and tomatoes tossed with tagliatelle, a generous amount of butter and loads of black pepper. Chicken livers are easy to cook and their preparation is minimal.

Duck has a very rich flavour due to its fat content. I find the best part tends to be the legs, as they don't dry out like the breast does and have a much nicer texture when cooked and shredded. One of my favourite recipes in this book is Pappardelle with Braised Duck, Peaches, Cinnamon and Cream (see page 189). Try this dish when peaches are at their best.

Most poultry and game is widely available from butchers around the country. Game is very seasonal, however, so try to make these dishes at the correct time of year. Alternatively, pheasant, partridge and pigeon all freeze quite well.

Agnolotti with Pigeon

Agnolotti is one of the most rustic filled pastas, and one of the easiest to make. The important thing with any stuffed pasta is to ensure that the filling is well seasoned and the flavours quite concentrated.

If you are lucky enough to get hold of a white or even a black truffle, a few shavings make this a very, very luxurious dish.

2 squab or wood pigeon
3 tablespoons marsala
1 teaspoon thyme
1 tablespoon olive oil
75g pancetta, finely diced
1 celery stick, finely diced
1 small onion, finely diced
1 small carrot, finely diced
½ glass of white wine
100g Parmesan cheese, freshly grated
½ quantity of Pasta Dough (see page 13)
75g unsalted butter
sea salt and freshly ground black pepper

Using a sharp knife, cut along the backbone of each bird and then open it out flat like a book. Put in a shallow dish, sprinkle over the marsala and thyme and leave to marinate for 1 hour.

Heat the olive oil in a large casserole, add the pigeons and brown lightly all over. Remove and set aside. Add the diced pancetta, celery, onion and carrot to the pan and cook for 2–3 minutes, until softened. Return the birds to the pan, add the white wine and some seasoning, then cover with foil or a tight-fitting lid and place in an oven preheated to 160°C/Gas Mark 3. Cook for about an hour, until the birds are very tender, then leave to cool.

Discard the skin and bones from the pigeon and finely chop the meat, putting it in a bowl. Drain all the liquid from the pan and set aside. Chop the pancetta, carrot, onion and celery to a fine mince and mix with the pigeon. Add the Parmesan, season to taste and add enough of the cooking liquid to give a moist but not wet mixture. Be careful, as if the filling is too wet the pasta will break up during cooking.

Roll out the pasta dough and make the agnolotti as described on page 17. Cook in a large pan of boiling salted water for 2–3 minutes, until *al dente*. Meanwhile, soften the butter in a large frying pan, but don't let it melt completely. Drain the pasta, add to the frying pan and toss gently until coated with the butter, giving a shiny appearance. Serve in bowls, with black pepper and a glass of Chianti.

Rigatoni with Rabbit, Pancetta and Rosemary

Rabbit has a fairly mild flavour, so it's always advisable to cook something like pancetta or prosciutto with it. This recipe uses pancetta and a soffritto (a base of finely chopped carrot, celery and onion) to give a good background flavour. The tomatoes and the addition of a little cream emulsify the rabbit's cooking juices to create a sauce that will lightly coat the rigatoni.

1 tablespoon olive oil
2 rabbit legs
2 small carrots, finely chopped
1 celery stick, finely chopped
1 small red onion, finely chopped
75g sliced pancetta
400g can of chopped tomatoes
a sprig of rosemary
150ml white wine
1 tablespoon double cream
400g rigatoni
sea salt and freshly ground black pepper
freshly grated Parmesan cheese, to serve

Heat the olive oil in a saucepan, add the rabbit legs and cook until browned all over. Remove and set aside. Add the chopped carrots, celery, onion and pancetta and cook slowly for 3–4 minutes, until the vegetables have softened. Stir in the chopped tomatoes, rosemary and white wine and simmer for 5 minutes, until slightly reduced. Return the rabbit legs to the saucepan, cover with a lid and cook gently for 45 minutes or until the rabbit meat is tender enough to come away from the bone easily. Take the rabbit legs out of the sauce and strip all the meat off them in small shreds. Return it to the sauce, season well and stir in the double cream.

Cook the rigatoni in a large pan of boiling salted water until *al dente*. Drain and add to the sauce. Toss well, cook gently for 2 minutes, then serve with black pepper and some freshly grated Parmesan.

Pappardelle with Braised Duck, Peaches, Cinnamon and Cream

This may sound like an odd combination but sweet fruit and duck always go well together. The addition of cinnamon makes the sauce almost fragrant, but it doesn't take away the richness of the slow-cooked duck.

1 tablespoon olive oil
2 duck legs
1 tablespoon chopped celery
1 tablespoon chopped red onion
75g pancetta, cut into matchsticks
1 ripe peach, skinned, stoned and chopped
¼ cinnamon stick
½ glass of white wine
1 tablespoon double cream
250g fresh pappardelle (or dried egg pappardelle)
sea salt and freshly ground black pepper
freshly grated Parmesan cheese, to serve (optional)

Heat the oil in a heavy-based casserole, add the duck legs and brown them all over, then remove from the pan. Add the celery, onion and pancetta to the pan and cook gently until softened. Return the duck legs to the pan, add the peach, cinnamon and white wine, then cover the pan tightly with foil, making sure there are no gaps. Transfer to an oven preheated to 160°C/Gas Mark 3 and cook for about 1½ hours, or until the duck meat comes away from the bone easily.

When the duck is cool enough to handle, discard the fat and skin, remove all the meat from the bones and tear it into small pieces. Skim off the excess fat from the pan and stir all the duck meat into the juices. Season to taste, then stir in the double cream and reheat gently.

Cook the pappardelle in a large pan of boiling salted water for 3–4 minutes, until *al dente* (or cook according to the packet instructions for dried pappardelle). Drain, reserving a few spoonfuls of the cooking water, and add to the duck and peach sauce. Toss well, adding a little of the reserved pasta water if necessary to loosen the sauce, then cook over a low heat for 2 minutes. Serve with black pepper and, if you like, a little Parmesan.

Orecchiette with Duck

You don't have to buy a whole duck for this dish. It's much better made using the legs rather than the breasts, because the meat is juicier and has more flavour. It's also a lot cheaper.

When you cook the orecchiette, make sure it's not too *al dente,* as it's a very dense pasta and takes longer than you might think to cook through to the centre.

1 tablespoon olive oil
2 duck legs
100g smoked pancetta, finely chopped
1 onion, finely chopped
1 carrot, finely chopped
2 celery sticks, finely chopped
1 teaspoon chopped rosemary
400g can of chopped tomatoes
a glass of red wine, preferably Valpolicella
400g orecchiette
sea salt and freshly ground black pepper

Heat the oil in a heavy-based casserole, add the duck legs and brown them all over. Remove from the pan and set aside. Add the pancetta, onion, carrot and celery to the pan and cook until the vegetables have softened. Stir in the rosemary, tomatoes and red wine, then return the duck legs to the pan. Bring to the boil and season. Cover the casserole, place in an oven preheated to 160°C/ Gas Mark 3 and cook for about 1½ hours, until the duck meat comes away from the bone easily. Take out the duck legs, remove the fat and skin, rip off the meat in small pieces and set to one side. With a spoon, skim off the excess fat from the casserole – there will be quite a lot, as duck is generally very fatty. Return the duck meat to the pan, mash everything together and season to taste. Reheat gently.

Cook the orecchiette in a large pan of boiling salted water until *al dente*, then drain, reserving a little of the cooking water, and add to the sauce. Leave to cook on the stove for 2–3 minutes so the flavours of the sauce can be absorbed by the pasta. If the sauce appears very concentrated, add a little of the reserved pasta water. Toss well so each disc of orecchiette has a bit of sauce in its dimple, then serve with a glass of red wine, preferably Valpolicella Superiore.

Tagliatelle alla Romana

This is a true classic that you'll find in every trattoria in Rome. It's delicious and not expensive, as chicken livers are very reasonably priced.

35g unsalted butter
2 tablespoons olive oil
I small red onion, finely chopped
200g fresh chicken livers
400g can of chopped tomatoes
250g fresh tagliatelle (or dried egg tagliatelle)
sea salt and freshly ground black pepper

Melt half the butter in a large saucepan or a deep frying pan and add the olive oil. Once it is hot, add the onion and cook until softened but not coloured. Season the chicken livers with salt and pepper, add to the pan and cook until light golden. Add the tomatoes and cook over a low heat for 20 minutes, stirring occasionally. Remove the chicken livers with a slotted spoon, chop finely, then return them to the pan. Stir well and season to taste.

Cook the tagliatelle in a large pan of boiling salted water for about 3 minutes, until *al dente* (or cook according to the packet instructions for dried tagliatelle). Drain and add to the sauce, along with the remaining butter. Toss well and cook gently for 2 minutes to ensure the pasta absorbs the flavours of the sauce. Serve immediately, with generous amounts of black pepper.

Ravioli with Pheasant, Tomato, Ricotta and Roasting Juices

Always try to use a hen pheasant, because girls tend to be more tender than boys. The cooking juices from the pheasant, combined with tomatoes, marsala and a little cream, make a delicious sauce for the ravioli.

1 hen pheasant
2 tablespoons olive oil
1 tablespoon finely chopped celery
1 tablespoon finely chopped carrot
1 tablespoon finely chopped onion
75g pancetta, cut into matchsticks
1 teaspoon thyme
100ml dry marsala
400g can of chopped tomatoes
250g ricotta cheese
½ quantity of Pasta Dough (see page 13)
50ml double cream
sea salt and freshly ground black pepper
freshly grated Parmesan cheese, to serve

Season the pheasant with salt and pepper. Heat the olive oil in a large casserole, add the pheasant and brown it on all sides. Take it out of the pan and set aside. Add the celery, carrot, onion, pancetta and thyme to the pan and cook gently until softened. Add the marsala and simmer for 2 minutes, until slightly reduced, then add the tomatoes and return the pheasant to the pan. Cover with foil or a tight-fitting lid and transfer to an oven preheated to 160°C/Gas Mark 3. Cook for 1 hour and 20 minutes or until the pheasant is tender and the meat comes away from the carcass easily. Take it out of the casserole, leave to cool, then take off the breast and legs and tear all the meat off them. Chop it up finely and leave to one side. Put the casserole back on the stove and add a teacup of water to the tomato, marsala and pancetta mixture. Bring to the boil and season to taste. Remove half the cooking juices from this sauce, put them in a large bowl, then add the chopped pheasant and the ricotta and mix well. Adjust the seasoning.

Roll out the pasta dough and make the ravioli as described on page 16, filling them with the pheasant and ricotta mixture. Add the double cream to the leftover sauce in the casserole, reheat gently and check the seasoning. Add the ravioli to a large pan of boiling salted water and simmer for 3–5 minutes, until *al dente*. Drain and add to the sauce. Serve with grated Parmesan and black pepper.

Pappardelle with Partridge, Pancetta, Tomato and Mascarpone

I recommend grey partridge, if you can get them. They are native British birds and are generally wild, making them more flavoursome than the widely farmed French red-leg partridge. The addition of Nebbiolo wine gives this dish a lovely, wintry feel.

2 tablespoons olive oil
2 grey partridge or red-leg partridge, cut in half
1 tablespoon chopped celery
1 tablespoon chopped carrot
1 tablespoon chopped onion
75g pancetta, cut into matchsticks
1 teaspoon chopped rosemary
150ml red wine, Nebbiolo if possible
400g can of chopped tomatoes
2 tablespoons mascarpone cheese
250g fresh pappardelle (or dried egg pappardelle)
sea salt and freshly ground black pepper
freshly grated Parmesan cheese, to serve

Heat the olive oil in a heavy-based casserole, add the partridge and brown them on all sides. Remove from the pan and set aside. Add the celery, carrot, onion, pancetta and rosemary to the pan and cook gently for 5 minutes, until the vegetables have softened. Add the red wine and simmer for 2 minutes, until slightly reduced. Stir in the tomatoes, bring to the boil, then return the birds to the casserole. Cover with foil or a tight-fitting lid, transfer to an oven preheated to 160°C/Gas Mark 3 and cook for 45 minutes or until the meat is tender and comes away from the carcass easily. Remove the partridges from the casserole and let them cool down. Cut off the breasts and legs and pull the meat off them, discarding the skin. Return the meat to the casserole and gently reheat the sauce. Stir in the mascarpone and season to taste.

Cook the pappardelle in a large pan of boiling salted water for 3–4 minutes, until *al dente* (or cook according to the packet instructions for dried pappardelle). Drain and toss with the sauce. Cook over a low heat for a couple of minutes, then serve with black pepper and some grated Parmesan.

Cheese

Cheese

This chapter contains some of the quickest and simplest recipes in the book. Many of them involve little or no cooking, relying on cheese as a main ingredient to sauce the pasta. Try Linguine with Mozzarella, Rocket and Anchovy (see page 202). You simply mix the ingredients together while the pasta is cooking – perfect for baking-hot summer days. Cheese is inseparable from pasta in many people's minds, as it provides the final seasoning for so many dishes, and Parmesan is considered indispensable for this very reason. In Italy it is regarded as the king of cheeses – because of its size, its cost and the rigorous controls that are applied to its production. The name parmigiano reggiano is a guarantee of quality and proves that the cheese has been made to certain specifications in the Emilia Romagna region and aged for 18 to 24 months. Made from cow's milk, it has a strong, nutty flavour and can vary greatly from farm to farm. Some make up to 300 wheels a day, while others produce only 5 or 6. The latter are likely to be 100 per cent handmade and therefore more flavoursome. One way of guaranteeing a quality product is to buy organic Parmesan, because it won't have been mass produced and the cows will have been fed a natural diet. When stored properly – wrapped in greaseproof paper and then sealed in a bag to stop it drying out – Parmesan will keep in the fridge for months, if you can resist eating it. Be careful not to be too generous with it in cooking, however, as it can become quite overpowering and very rich. Used subtly, it has fantastic seasoning qualities for a simple pasta dish, such as tagliatelle with butter and black pepper.

A lesser-known cheese that deserves more attention outside Italy is pecorino, which is made from sheep's milk. Simple and creamy, it is one of Italy's most prized cheeses, as it's made all over the country but each region has its own special version.

On a recent trip to Puglia, I was inspired by the use of buffalo mozzarella and burrata, which were served not as a garnish but as a seasoning on the pasta, very simply presented. What makes this particularly good is that you have the hot pasta underneath and the cool mozzarella or burrata on top, with its gorgeous, creamy flavour.

Mascarpone is a really versatile cheese. A mixture of cheese and cream, it's very rich but you need to use only a little in cooking as it is so dense. A small amount added to pasta sauces emulsifies them and brings all the flavours together.

My favourite cheese of all is gorgonzola, as it has a deliciously nutty, salty taste. In small quantities, it brings out the flavour of any pasta dish – try Tagliatelle with Gorgonzola and Radicchio (page 210) and you will see what I mean.

Linguine with Mozzarella, Rocket and Anchovy

This is the quickest pasta dish on earth, and definitely one of the tastiest. *(See picture, opposite.)*

4 salted anchovy fillets in olive oil, very finely chopped
1 tablespoon chopped flat-leaf parsley
150g buffalo mozzarella, cut into small pieces
100g wild rocket, chopped
4 tablespoons olive oil
400g linguine
sea salt and freshly ground black pepper

Mix the anchovies, parsley, mozzarella and rocket together in a large bowl. Season with black pepper and stir in half the olive oil.

Cook the linguine in a large pan of boiling salted water until *al dente,* then drain. Add to the anchovy mixture and toss together so the mozzarella melts. Season, drizzle the remaining oil on top and serve immediately.

Spaghetti with Lemon, Basil, Olive Oil and Parmesan

Fast food doesn't have to be tasteless, greasy and bad for you. It can also mean simple, delicious pasta dishes, such as this one, which has very few ingredients. The sauce can be prepared in the time it takes to cook the pasta.

400g spaghetti
120ml good olive oil
juice of 3 lemons
100g Parmesan cheese, freshly grated
a bunch of basil
salt and freshly ground black pepper

Cook the spaghetti in a large pan of boiling salted water until *al dente.* Meanwhile, whisk the olive oil and lemon juice together in a large bowl, gradually adding the grated Parmesan. The mixture should emulsify. Season to taste.

Drain the spaghetti and add it to the bowl containing the sauce. Rip up the basil and add to the pasta with plenty of black pepper. Toss together and serve immediately.

Tagliatelle with Pecorino, Cream, Spinach and Marjoram

Pecorino is a sheep's milk cheese and comes in various incarnations: sweet, salty, and even with a touch of chilli. The best pecorinos for cooking tend to be the young ones, as they haven't lost that fresh, creamy taste. The problem with having pecorino in your fridge is that it is so good you usually eat it before you can use it for your pasta.

500g fresh spinach
50g unsalted butter
1 garlic clove, finely sliced
2 teaspoons chopped marjoram
100ml double cream
250g fresh tagliatelle (or dried egg tagliatelle)
100g pecorino cheese, grated
sea salt and freshly ground black pepper

Put the spinach in a large pan of boiling salted water and cook for 1 minute. Strain through a colander and leave to cool. Squeeze out the excess water and chop the spinach finely.
Melt the butter in a large, heavy-based frying pan, add the garlic and cook gently until soft. Add the marjoram and cook for 1 minute, then stir in the spinach and cook for 2–3 minutes. Add the double cream, season and cook for a further 2 minutes.

Cook the tagliatelle in a large pan of boiling salted water for about 3 minutes, until *al dente* (or cook according to the packet instructions for dried tagliatelle). Drain, reserving a few spoonfuls of the cooking water, and toss with the sauce, adding half the pecorino at this point. Add a little of the reserved pasta water to loosen the sauce if necessary, then cook gently for a minute or so. Serve with black pepper and the remaining pecorino on the side.

Spaghetti with Parmesan, Olives, Basil and Cream

This recipe uses Taggiasche olives, which come from Liguria. You could use any small black olives, but make sure they have been in brine and nothing else, as you want the natural olive flavour to be the predominant taste here.

A useful tip when stoning olives is to place them on a tea towel and push down on them with a ramekin or a teacup to flatten them. This makes it easy to take the flesh off the stones.

150g Taggiasche olives, stoned
½ garlic clove, peeled
8 basil leaves
1 tablespoon olive oil
100ml double cream
400g spaghetti
75g Parmesan cheese, freshly grated, plus extra to serve
sea salt and freshly ground black pepper

Place the olives on a board with the garlic and basil and chop as finely as you can. Heat the oil in a large frying pan, add the chopped olive mixture and cook gently for 3–4 minutes. Stir in the double cream and cook for a further 4 minutes.

Meanwhile, cook the spaghetti in a large pan of boiling salted water until *al dente*. Drain, reserving a little of the cooking water, and toss with the olives and cream. Add the Parmesan, then thin the sauce with a tablespoon or two of the pasta cooking water if necessary. Check the seasoning; you might find it's seasoned enough because of the saltiness of the olives. Toss well and serve with black pepper and more Parmesan.

Tagliatelle with Pesto

I was taught to make pesto by Lorenzo Shiffini, a chef from Liguria, who told me that making it in a blender is the best way because it doesn't discolour and the basil is completely puréed, releasing all of its flavour. It also emulsifies everything so it doesn't become too lumpy. Interestingly enough, he added a few tablespoons of water, which brings out the flavour of the basil. It was the best pesto I've ever tasted, because it wasn't oily and heavy, it simply tasted of basil and seasoning.

a generous bunch of basil (about 150g)
75g pine nuts (preferably European ones)
100g Parmesan cheese, freshly grated, plus extra to serve
3 tablespoons water
1 garlic clove, crushed with a little sea salt
6 tablespoons olive oil
250g fresh tagliatelle (or dried egg tagliatelle)
sea salt and freshly ground black pepper

Remove all the basil leaves from their stalks, wash them thoroughly and place in a blender. Add the pine nuts, Parmesan, water and crushed garlic and switch on the blender; everything should turn bright green. Turn it off, add the olive oil and blitz again for 20 seconds. Remove the mixture from the blender, season to taste and put to one side.

Cook the tagliatelle in a large pan of boiling salted water for about 3 minutes, until *al dente* (or cook according to the packet instructions for dried tagliatelle), then drain. Put the pesto in a large frying pan, warm it gently, then stir in the pasta. Serve with grated Parmesan and some black pepper.

Spaghetti with Burrata, Tomatoes and Basil

Burrata is mozzarella that has been stretched and filled with fresh cream. It is very delicate and best eaten as soon as it is made. You can get burrata in the UK, but if you can't find it, use good buffalo mozzarella instead.

2 tablespoons olive oil
1 garlic clove, finely sliced
300g fresh plum tomatoes, skinned and chopped
8 basil leaves, torn
400g spaghetti
150g burrata cheese
sea salt and freshly ground black pepper
good olive oil, to serve

Heat the olive oil in a large frying pan, add the garlic and cook gently until soft. Add the chopped tomatoes and cook rapidly for 5–7 minutes, until the sauce has thickened and the flavour is concentrated. Stir in the basil and season to taste.

Cook the spaghetti in a large pan of boiling salted water until *al dente*, then drain. Add to the tomato sauce, toss well and adjust the seasoning. Add half the burrata, cut into small lumps – you can just scoop out lumps with a spoon, if you like. Toss again and serve with the remaining burrata on each portion, finishing with black pepper and a dash of some really good olive oil on the burrata.

Tagliatelle with Gorgonzola and Radicchio

This is definitely a winter pasta. As the radicchio cooks down, it loses its bitterness and the flavour becomes more concentrated. With the robust, creamy, tangy gorgonzola, it makes a truly delicious sauce.

Gorgonzola is also lovely eaten on its own with ripe pears. Try to buy it from a cheese shop rather than pre-sliced and ready wrapped, because invariably the pre-packed cheeses are cut before they are ripe, making them easier to package.

1 tablespoon olive oil
1 garlic clove, finely sliced
½ teaspoon chopped rosemary
1 head of radicchio, shredded
75g mascarpone cheese
250g fresh tagliatelle (or dried egg tagliatelle)
100g gorgonzola naturale (also known as gorgonzola piccante)
sea salt and freshly ground black pepper

Heat the olive oil in a large, heavy-based frying pan, add the garlic and cook gently until soft. Add the rosemary and then the shredded radicchio and cook for about 15 minutes, until the radicchio has completely wilted and is very soft. Stir in the mascarpone and season to taste.

Cook the tagliatelle in a large pan of boiling salted water for about 3 minutes, until *al dente* (or cook according to the packet instructions for dried tagliatelle). Drain, reserving a few spoonfuls of the cooking water, and add to the radicchio sauce. Crumble in the gorgonzola, leaving a few large lumps. Adjust the seasoning, but be careful, because gorgonzola can be a bit salty. Toss well, add a little of the reserved pasta water to loosen the sauce, if necessary, then cook over a low heat for 2 minutes. Serve with black pepper and a good glass of Valpolicella or, better still, Amarone.

Rigatoni with Parmesan, Cream, Parma Ham and Egg

If this recipe sounds rich, it is, but it is utterly delicious, as long as you don't overcook the egg.

75g unsalted butter
150g Parma ham, cut into strips
100ml double cream
3 organic egg yolks
a pinch of grated nutmeg
400g rigatoni
75g Parmesan cheese, freshly grated
sea salt and freshly ground black pepper

Melt the butter in a large frying pan, add the Parma ham and cook gently until lightly coloured. Take the pan off the heat – don't worry about the fat, it adds flavour. Add the cream, egg yolks and nutmeg and mix together so they emulsify.

Cook the rigatoni in a large pan of boiling salted water until *al dente*, then drain. Put the Parma ham mixture back on the heat, add the rigatoni and toss together over a low heat for a minute or two, so the sauce coats the pasta. Add the Parmesan, toss again and season to taste. Serve with black pepper and a little more Parmesan if required.

Tagliatelle with Pecorino, Butter and Sage

This is another very simple pasta dish. Try to find a Tuscan pecorino, as they have a lovely, creamy flavour and are not too salty.

100g unsalted butter
8 large sage leaves
250g fresh tagliatelle (or dried egg tagliatelle)
100g pecorino toscano cheese, grated
freshly ground black pepper

Melt the butter in a large frying pan and add the sage. Turn off the heat and leave to infuse for 5 minutes. Meanwhile, cook the tagliatelle in a large pan of boiling salted water for about 3 minutes, until *al dente* (or cook according to the packet instructions for dried tagliatelle). Drain but keep a little of the cooking water. Add the tagliatelle to the frying pan, then add the pecorino and 2–3 tablespoons of the reserved cooking water. Toss together over a medium heat so the cheese coats the pasta, then serve with black pepper.

Penne with Lemon, Parmesan, Cream and Rocket

You must try this recipe if you have some good lemons. In the restaurant we always use the large Amalfi lemons. Try to avoid waxed ones, as they will not have the ultra-lemony flavour that you get from Amalfi lemons in particular. Be generous with the Parmesan here.

1 large unwaxed lemon
150ml double cream
100g wild rocket, chopped
400g penne rigate
100g Parmesan cheese, freshly grated
sea salt and freshly ground black pepper

Remove the zest from the lemon in long strips, using a potato peeler. Heat the double cream in a large frying pan, then squeeze in the lemon juice and add the zest. Cook gently for 2–3 minutes. Remove the lemon zest and add the rocket to the pan. Turn off the heat and season to taste.

Cook the penne in a large pan of boiling salted water until *al dente*. Drain, reserving a little of the cooking water, and add to the cream, rocket and lemon. Toss together, then add the Parmesan and a couple of spoonfuls of the reserved cooking water. Serve with loads of black pepper and more Parmesan if required.

Tagliatelle with Crème Fraîche, Parmesan and Asparagus

This pasta sauce is particularly rich, as it's made using egg yolks, crème fraîche and Parmesan, but it's a great way of eating the new season's English asparagus. Try to use select asparagus, which is medium thickness, as it has a lovely, tender texture.

400ml crème fraîche
1 garlic clove, crushed to a paste with a little salt
3 organic egg yolks
150g Parmesan cheese, freshly grated, plus extra to serve
250g fresh tagliatelle
300g medium-thick asparagus spears, trimmed and finely sliced at an angle
sea salt and freshly ground black pepper

Put the crème fraîche, garlic, egg yolks and Parmesan in a large bowl and set it over a pan of simmering water, making sure the water does not touch the base of the bowl. Whisk vigorously with a balloon whisk until the mixture is the consistency of runny honey; it should be thick enough to coat the back of a spoon. Check the seasoning, then put to one side.

Put the tagliatelle and asparagus in a large pan of boiling salted water and cook for 3 minutes or until the pasta is *al dente*. Drain and toss with the crème fraîche and Parmesan sauce. Serve with plenty of black pepper and more Parmesan on top.

Spaghetti with Pecorino, Black Pepper and Butter

This classic dish is popular in most parts of Italy. It is very simple but, made well, can be amazingly delicious.

400g spaghetti
75g unsalted butter
150g pecorino toscano cheese, grated
freshly ground black pepper

Put the spaghetti in a large pan of boiling salted water and cook until *al dente*. Meanwhile, melt the butter in a large frying pan. Remove from the heat, add the pecorino cheese and grind in plenty of black pepper. And I mean plenty!

When the spaghetti is cooked, drain, keeping a little of the pasta water, and add to the butter and pecorino. Toss very well, adding a few spoonfuls of the pasta water to help emulsify the sauce. The spaghetti should be coated in the cheese so it looks like a cheese sauce. Serve immediately, with some more black pepper if you like.

Ravioli with Sheep's Ricotta, Lemon and Peas

Sheep's milk ricotta has more flavour than cow's milk ricotta, but if you can't get hold of it you could use the cow's milk version here. Try not to use the commercial small tubs, as double cream is added to these to make it thicker.

If the peas are small and tender, they should take the same time to cook as the ravioli. If not, cook them beforehand and just blanch them with the ravioli – or you can use frozen peas but they will not be as good.

500g sheep's milk ricotta cheese
100g pecorino toscano cheese, grated, plus extra to serve
juice and grated zest of 1 lemon
½ quantity of Pasta Dough (see page 13)
200g shelled fresh peas
75g unsalted butter
sea salt and freshly ground black pepper

Put the ricotta in a large bowl, add the pecorino and the lemon juice and zest and mix well. Season to taste.

Roll out the pasta and make the ravioli as described on page 16. Add the ravioli and peas to a large pan of boiling salted water and simmer for 3 or 4 minutes, until the pasta is *al dente*. Meanwhile, soften the butter in a large frying pan, but don't let it melt completely. Drain the ravioli and peas and add them to the butter. Season and serve with black pepper and a little more grated pecorino.

Pansotti with Ricotta, Fennel Tops and Walnut Sauce

Pansotti is a half-moon-shaped pasta. Here it is stuffed with a light and delicious combination of sheep's ricotta and fennel. Serving it with walnut sauce makes it a much more luxurious and textural dish. If you have any sauce left over, it is very good served with tagliatelle.

The best ricotta is made from sheep's milk, as it has a much sweeter flavour and better texture than cow's milk ricotta. The shelf life of cow's milk ricotta is three times as long as that of a sheep's ricotta, however, making it much more readily available – this is the variety you are able to buy in most shops in sealed tubs. Sheep's milk ricotta is available in the UK only in specialist cheese shops and must be used immediately.

200g ricotta cheese (preferably sheep's milk ricotta)
2 tablespoons chopped fennel tops (i.e. the feathery top of the bulb) or, better still, fennel herb
½ quantity of Pasta Dough (see page 13)
50g unsalted butter
sea salt and freshly ground black pepper

For the walnut sauce:
½ garlic clove, peeled
100g walnuts
juice of ½ lemon
75g Parmesan cheese, freshly grated
2 tablespoons full-fat milk
4 tablespoons olive oil
1 teaspoon chopped parsley

To make the filling, beat the ricotta and fennel together in a bowl and season to taste.

To make the walnut sauce, crush the garlic with a pinch of sea salt in a pestle and mortar, then add the walnuts. Pound until smooth, then mix in the lemon juice, Parmesan, milk, olive oil, and parsley, one after the other. Work this mixture together so the sauce becomes emulsified, then check the seasoning.

Roll out the pasta dough in a strip 60cm long and 12cm wide (see page 13). Place heaped teaspoons of the filling along the length of the pasta, leaving a 3cm gap between each one and making sure there is enough pasta free to fold over the filling. Brush between each portion of filling with a pastry brush dipped in water, then fold the pasta over and, using your 2 little fingers, push down round each pile of filling to seal. Try to make sure that there is no trapped air inside or the pasta will burst during cooking.

Use a round pastry cutter placed around the filling, half on and half off the pasta (see photo), to cut out half-moon shapes. Pick them up individually to make sure each one is airtight. They will keep in the fridge on a floured tray for up to 2 days, or you can cook them immediately.

Cook the pansotti in a large pan of boiling salted water for 3–4 minutes, until *al dente*. Meanwhile, melt the butter in a large frying pan. Drain the pasta, add to the frying pan and toss together. Add a generous spoonful of the walnut sauce and toss again. Add a good grind of black pepper and serve, with extra walnut sauce if desired.

INDEX

ACKNOWLEDGEMENTS

Huge thanks to Maria Wrazen, Sarah Lavelle, Vanessa Courtier, Wei Tang, Fiona Lindsey, Mary Bekhait, Carey Smith, Fiona MacIntyre, Theodore Hill, Luis Rodriguez, David Okogie, Taheer Tawal, Sanjeewa Thommadura, Hazel Griffiths, Gilberto Souza, Chris Beverly, Louisa Bradford, Nicholas Shizas, Joseph Lanfranchi, Ben Richardson, Alison Stubberfield, Manuel Toews, Ophelie Griffond, Liis Tiisvelt, Lazhar Abdessamed, Rada Djerasimovic, Hans Schauhuber, Vanina Stanek, Vitali Birjukov, Juraj Cako, MarianOntko, Paul Bates and Franco Fabini. Also to Peter Randall, Rosemary Randall, Claudia Randall and Justine Randall.

ABOUT THE AUTHOR

Theo Randall, who served his apprenticeship with Max Magarian in London and Alice Waters in San Francisco, was head chef at the Michelin-starred River Café for ten years. He now runs his own restaurant, Theo Randall at the InterContinental Park Lane, in London. Theo lives in London with his wife Natalie and two children, Max and Lola.

Bucatini ▶

◀ Linguine

Penne rigate ▶

Farfalle ▼

◀ Pennette

Cannolichi ▶

Stracci ▶

Spaghetti ▶

Vermicelli ▲

Tagliatelle ▼

Cavatelli ▶